# CHRISTIANITY
*Before*
# CHRIST

# CHRISTIANITY
## *Before*
# CHRIST

John G. Jackson

With a Foreword by Frank R. Zindler

American Atheist Press **AAP** Austin, Texas 1985

Illustrations by Gerald Tholen

American Atheist Press,
P.O. Box 5733,
Parsippany, NJ 07054-6733

ISBN 0-910309-20-5

# TABLE OF CONTENTS

# Illustrations

# FOREWORD

John G. Jackson's *Christianity Before Christ* has always
been one of the best-selling titles offered by American Atheist
Press. It is a much-loved Atheist classic that has been reprinted many times over the years. It is a work that the author
always sought to improve and bring into line with the best-
informed scholarly opinion of his day. Unfortunately, the death
of the author in the mid-1990s – shortly before the deaths of
the Murray-O'Hairs, the "First Family of American Atheism" –
froze the book in its present form, with no possibility of his
issuing an improved edition more accurately reflecting the
evolved scholarly opinion of the twenty-first century. When the
stockpile of books ran out in 2001, it became my responsibili-
ty to decide if American Atheist Press should reprint the book,
decline to reprint the book, or issue a mutilated new edition in
which each out-dated opinion would be footnoted with detailed
references to the latest findings and theories relating to each
point.

The long, enduring popularity of *Christianity Before
Christ* ruled out of bounds the option of just letting the book
die. On the other hand, the amount of research that would be
needed to check out the latest scholarly opinion concerning
every page of the book would impossibly overload an already
overworked editor and render ugly a book that so many have
loved for so long. Fortunately, almost all the points now being
called into question concern the precise antiquity of Egyptian
and other African cultural developments, as well as scholarly
understanding of the origins and purposes of the Giza
Pyramids. (And of course, our understanding of the evolutionary time-table has become much more precise since Jackson
wrote this book.)

According to the Afrocentric theory incorporated into
parts of this book, virtually everything began in Africa, and no
matter what the point in question, black Africans did it first.
Of course Jackson never embraced the theory in its extreme
form, but his own status as an American pioneer in African

Studies and founder of one of the first academic programs in Afro-American Studies made the blandishments of at least parts of Afrocentric theory irresistible.

Luckily, even if we reject those questionable details of *Christianity Before Christ*, the general thesis of the book remains unshaken, *viz.*, that *nothing* is new in Christianity. Its least important features, as well as its most important components, were all well developed in cultures that flourished well before the time that Christ is alleged to have walked the parched paths of Roman Palestine. The information presented in this book is absolutely crucial if Atheists and other free thinkers are to understand the nature of the beast that threatens not only their liberties and rights as citizens in a secular republic, but also threatens to return world civilization itself back to the prescientific levels of the ancient cultures from which Christianity derived all its odd details. Every Atheist needs to know what is in this book!

Potentially one of the most important topics discussed in this book is found as Chapter IV: Bel, The Babylonian Christ. In this chapter mention is made of a Babylonian tablet now in the British Museum that records a passion play in which the god Bel undergoes a trial, execution, and resurrection that is astonishingly similar in its details to the passion stories now found in the Christian New Testament. The Babylonian tablet is said to date from around 2000 BCE, and it would appear that the Christian passion story is merely a late edition of the Babylonian drama.

If it could be proved that something supposedly so unique and detailed as the Christian passion tale was merely an adaptation of a religious drama that was already over two millennia older than Christianity, the argument against the authenticity of Christianity could be strengthened several orders of magnitude. The notion that Jesus Christ was no more historical than Zeus, Osiris, Krishna, or Bel would be virtually proven.

Unfortunately, since John G. Jackson – for all his brilliance – was not an Assyriologist who could read cuneiform tablets on his own, he had to rely on secondary or even tertiary sources for his discussion of this most tantalizing topic. More unfortunately, his only source for information concerning the Babylonian passion play is a book by J. Arthur Findlay, *The Psychic Stream: or, the Source and Growth of the Christian Faith* (London: Psychic Press, 1947). According to Findlay, the Babylonian passion play is based on a tablet discussed in the ruins of Babylon by "Professor H. Zimmern," and the curator of the Babylonian Section of the British Museum supplied him with a translation of the document.

Now a publication by the Psychic Press is not likely to inspire much confidence on the part of Atheist scholars. Even so, it is unthinkable that Findlay simply made up the story – despite the fact that John G. Jackson appears to be the only other scholar to have examined it in fifty years. It is possible the story was just too hot for mainline scholars to handle.

Because of the extreme importance of this question, I myself have tried to discover the facts concerning the Babylonian Passion Play. Almost certainly, the "Professor H. Zimmern" was Heinrich Zimmern, a German Assyriologist who lived from 1862 to 1931. Zimmern published a number of books that certainly might relate to the subject in question. His *Babylonische Hymnen und Gebete* ('Babylonian Hymns and Prayers', 2 parts, 1905, 1911) and his *Vater, Sohn, und Fürsprecher in der Babylonischen Gottesvorstellung* ('Father, Son, and Intercessor in the Babylonian Conception of God', Leipzig, 1896) might certainly be expected to contain some reference to the tablet in question. Even more tantalizingly, he authored a work entitled *Zum Streit um die "Christusmythe"* ('The Christ-Myth Controversy'), relating to Arthur Drews' book *Die Christusmythe* ('The Christ Myth'), a work arguing that Jesus was not an historical figure.

Alas, as this book goes to press, I have been unable to obtain any of these rare books, and e-mails to the present curator of the Babylonian Collection at the British Museum have gone unacknowledged as well as unanswered. If I am ever able to learn the truth about the Passion Play of Bel, I will add it to this foreword. Most likely, the information will warrant an entire book!

Frank R. Zindler, Editor
American Atheist Press
June, 2002

**John G. Jackson**

# ABOUT THE AUTHOR

John G . Jackson was an educator, lecturer, author, and man of principle. He was born on April 1, 1907, into a family of Methodists. As he remembers now, he has been an Atheist since he could think. The family minister once asked him when he was small, "Who made you?" After some thought he replied from his own realization, "I don't know." He lived for fifty years in New York City, 1932 to 1977, lecturing at the "Ingersoll Forum" of the American Association for the Advancement of Atheism (from 1930 to 1955). During a parallel period he wrote articles for the *Truth Seeker* magazine. He was at the same time a writer and associate of the Rationalist Press Association in London, England, from 1932 to 1972.

Beginning in 1971 he became a lecturer in the Black Studies Department of Rutgers University, remaining there until 1973. From 1973 to 1977 he was a Visiting Professor at the University of New York. When he moved to Chicago he quickly became a Visiting Professor at Northeast Illinois University from 1977 to 1980. One of the courses which he taught was "Comparative Religion." His approach to that course was such that university officials cautioned him to "be more discreet." Another of his courses dealt with "Social Movements."

Jackson was ever a consistent friend of labor and was a member of the UAW, Dist. 65, AFL-CIO, for most of his life.

His books include *Introduction to African Civilizations; A Guide to the Study of African History, Ethiopia and the Origin of Civilization; Man, God and Civilization;* and best-selling *Pagan Origins of the Christ Myth.*

# Introduction

The title of this essay may appear to some to be paradoxical. They might ask: How could there be Christianity before Christ? The great African Church Father, St. Augustine, studied this question and answered as follows:

> That which is known as the Christian religion existed among the ancients, and never did not exist; from the beginning of the human race until the time when Christ came in the flesh, at which time the *true* religion, which *already* existed began to be called Christianity. *(Retractt. I, xiii,* cited by Dr. Alvin Boyd Kuhn in his *Shadow of The Third Century,* Elizabeth N.J.: Academy Press, 1949, p.3.)

The above passage was followed by the appended commentary:

> This astonishing declaration was made in the early fourth century of our era. It can be asserted with little chance of refutation that if this affirmation of the pious Augustine had not sunk out of sight, but had been kept in open view through the period of Western history, the whole course of that history would have been vastly altered for the better. It is only too likely the case that the obvious implications of the passage were of such a nature that its open exploitation was designedly frowned upon by the ecclesiastical authorities in every age. It held the kernel of a great truth the common knowledge of which would have been a stumbling block in the way of the perpetuation of priestly power over the general Christian mind. It would have provoked inquiry and disarmed the ecclesiastical prestige of much of its power.

The commentary further stated:

> For what is it that the Christian saint actually says? It stands as hardly less than a point-blank repudiation of all the chief asseverations on which the

structure of Christian tradition rests. Every child born to Christian parents in eighteen centuries has been indoctrinated with the unqualified belief that Christianity was completely new, and the first true, religion in world history; that it was vouchsafed to the world by God himself and brought to earth by the sole divine emissary ever commissioned to convey God's truth to mankind; that it flashed out amid the lingering murks of Pagan darkness as the first ray of true light to illumine the pathway of evolution for the safe treading of human feet. All previous religion was the superstitious product of primitive childishness of mind. Christianity was the first piercing of the long night of black heathenism by the benignant gift of God.

Finally, the commentary stated:

Augustine shatters this illusion and this jealously preserved phantom of blind credulity. From remotest antiquity, he asserts, there has always existed in the world the true religion. It illuminated the intellects of the most ancient Sages, Prophets, Priests and Kings. It built the foundation for every national religion, the tenets of which consisted of reformulation of its ubiquitous ageless principles of knowledge and wisdom. It went under a variety of designations: Hermeticism in ancient Egypt; Orphism in early Greece; Zoroastrianism in Persia; Brahmanism in India; Taoism in China; Shintoism in Japan and China. In no matter what garbled and perverted form, even tribal religionism fostered it. Mystery cultism dramatized and ritualized it in many lands. Social usages, all the round of annual festivals, chimney-corner tale and castle ballad, countryside legend and folklore carried it down the stream of time. Always it existed among men; never was it not present in the world. Hardly ever apprehended at its real value, its representations badly misconceived, its import warped and travestied at every turn in popular practice, it yet existed and came down to Augustine's day. (Kuhn, *Shadow,* pp. 3-4)

There is an extensive literature on the Pagan origins of Christianity. Most of these works, written by scholars for scholars, never reached the general reader. Students of comparative religion are familiar with such books as *Bible Myths and Their Parallels in Other Religions,* by T. W. Doane; *The Golden Bough* and *Folklore in The Old Testament,* by Sir James G. Frazer; *Pagan and Christian Creeds,* by Edward Carpenter; *Anacalypsis,* by Godfrey Higgins; *Ancient Egypt — The Light of The World,* by Gerald Massey; *The Signs and Symbols of Primordial Man,* by Dr. Albert Churchward; and *Did Jesus Live 100 B.C.?,* by G. R. S. Mead. Most of these books are out of print or difficult to obtain by laymen who are interested in this field of study. So the purpose of this treatise is to popularize the results of the research of the great scholars named, and a few others, whom we will meet as we proceed in this study.

**James Ussher (1581-1656)**

# Chapter I
# The Creation of The World and of Man

Archbishop James Ussher in 1630 announced that the world was created by god in the year 4004 B.C. *(Annals of The Ancient and New Testament,* London: 1650, cited by Andrew Dickson White, *A History of The Warfare of Science with Theology in Christendom,* Vol. I, New York: D. Appleton and Co., 1896, p.9). This date has been accepted by large numbers of orthodox Christians. A more precise estimate of the age of the earth was made by Dr. John Lightfoot [1602-1675], Vice-Chancellor of the University of Cambridge, who declared that:

> Heaven and earth, centre and circumference, were created all together, in the same instant...this work took place and man was created by the Trinity on October 23, 4004 B.C., at nine o'clock in the morning. (White, *History,* Vol. I, p. 256.)

This estimate was widely accepted for about two hundred years, then grave doubts were cast upon it by discoveries made in the Nile Valley and in Western Asia, as a great American historian noted:

> Within two centuries after Lightfoot's great biblical demonstration to the exact hour of creation, it was discovered that at that hour an exceedingly cultivated people, enjoying all the fruits of a highly developed civilization, had long been swarming in the great cities of Egypt, and that other nations hardly less advanced had at that time reached a high development in Asia. (White, *History,* Vol. I, pp. 9-10.)

During the middle ages the Christian god was anthropomorphic. As Professor White observed:

> Among those masses of cathedral sculpture which preserve so much of medieval theology, one frequently recurring group is noteworthy for its presentment of a time-honored doctrine regarding the origin of the universe. The Almighty, in human form, sits benignly, making the sun, moon, and stars, and hanging them

from the solid firmament which supports the "heaven above" and overarches the "earth beneath." The furrows of thought on the Creator's brow show that in this work he is obliged to contrive; the knotted muscles upon his arms show that he is obliged to toil; naturally, they, the sculptors and painters of the medieval and early modern period frequently represented him as the writers whose conceptions they embodied had done — as, on the seventh day, weary after thought and toil, enjoying well-earned repose and the plaudits of the hosts of heaven. (White, *History,* p. 1)

There are two stories of the creation of man in Genesis; one in Chapter I, and the other in Chapter II. These two accounts flatly contradict each other, and this has created a problem for true believers. We learn from the first three verses of Genesis, Chapter I, that after God created the heavens and the earth, he gave the command "Let there be Light, and there was Light." Then the light was called day and the darkness, night. This completed the first day's work. The second day's work was the creation of the firmament. In the third day, God brought forth the dry land, which he called the earth, and the waters, called the seas. Then the earth was made to produce grass, trees, etc. Thus ended the third day of creation. Next, the sun and moon were created and set in the firmament by God. This ended the fourth day. On the next day, God created great whales and other water animals and also winged fowl. This concluded the work of the fifth day. The sixth day completed the work of creation; God made all sorts of beasts, cattle, creeping things, and finally man, whom he created male and female in his own image. On the seventh day God rested from his labors, and the day was blessed and sanctified as the sabbath.

In this first narrative, God is said to have created the lower animals first, and then later on, human beings, both male and female. In the second account we are told that God created man first, the lower animals next, and last of all, woman, who was made from a rib extracted from man. In the first story the creator begins with fishes, then produces in turn birds and beasts, and finally man and woman. In the second tale, man comes first, and God then makes the lower animals, and finally woman. The most noticeable points of difference between the two cosmogonies are:

(1) In the first, the earth emerged from the waters and was hence saturated with moisture. In the second, the whole face of the ground required moistening.

(2) In the first, the birds and beasts were created before man. In the second, man was created before the birds and beasts.

(3) In the first, all flying fowl were made from the waters. In the second, the fowl of the air were made out of the ground.

(4) In the first, man was made in the image of God. In the second, man was made from dust and then animated with the breath of life. After the eating of the forbidden fruit by the first human pair, the Lord God said, "Behold, the man has become *as one of us* to know good and evil."

(5) In the first, man was made lord of the *whole earth*. In the second, he was placed in the Garden of Eden only, to dress it and keep it.

(6) In the first, the man and woman were created together, as the closing work of the creation. In the second, man was created, then the birds and beasts, and lastly the woman was made from a rib of the man.

The discrepancies pointed out above are due to the fact that the first and second accounts were taken from two different documents. In the first narrative the creator is called Elohim (God) whereas in the second he is called Jehovah Elohim (Lord God). This fact was well expressed by Frazer as follows:

> The flagrant contradiction between the two accounts is explained very simply by the circumstance that they are derived from two different and originally independent documents, which were afterwards combined into a single book by an editor, who pieced the two narratives together without always taking pains to soften or harmonize their discrepancies. The account of the creation in the first chapter is derived from what is called the Priestly Document, which was composed by priestly writers during or

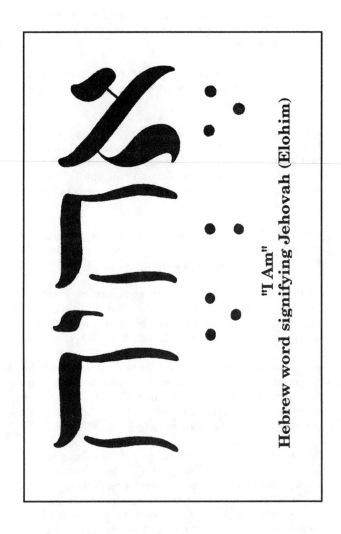

"I Am"
Hebrew word signifying Jehovah (Elohim)

after the Babylonian captivity. The account of the creation of man and the animals in the second chapter is derived from what is called the Jehovistic Document, which was written several hundred years before the other, probably in the ninth or eighth century before our era. (Sir James Frazer, *Folklore in The Old Testament,* Abridged Edition, New York: Hart Publishing Co., 1975, p.2.)

There are numerous parallels to the Genesis stories in the mythologies of many ancient peoples, and I shall briefly recount a few of them for purposes of comparison. The Jehovistic story told of how god fashioned the first man of clay, as a potter might do. Then, having kneaded the model into proper shape, the deity animated it with his breath. The first man was called Adam. In the ancient Hebrew language the word for man was *Adam,* the word for ground was *Adamah;* so, man was derived from the ground, or earth.

Among the Shilluks of the White Nile in Africa there is a myth explaining the various complexions of the human race. Juok, the creator, traveled over the world. He made black men out of black earth in the land of the Shilluks; in Egypt, he made brown men out of the mud of the Nile; out of white earth he made white men, and so on. Juok went about his creative work by taking a lump of earth, and saying,

> I will make man, but he must be able to walk and run and go out into the fields, so I will give him two long legs, like the flamingo. The man must be able to cultivate his millet, so I will give him two arms, one to hold the hoe, and the other to tear up the weeds. The man must be able to see his millet, so I will give him two eyes. The man must be able to eat his millet, so I will give him a mouth. The man must be able to dance and speak and sing and shout, and for these purposes he must have a tongue. The man must be able to hear the noise of the dance and the speech of great men, and for that he needs two ears.

So the Creator acted accordingly, finished his task, and sent the first man out into the world.

In the Egyptian creation myths, we are told that the universe came out of a cosmic egg.

In the version known at Memphis, in Egypt, Ptah (the Opener) broke the egg from which the sun and moon came forth. At Elephantine, the creation of the world was attributed to Knum, who molded the first man out of the mud of the Nile, like a potter working with his wheel. (Ernest Busenbark, *Symbols, Sex and The Stars*, New York: The Truth Seeker Co., 1949, p. 101.)

It is interesting to note that Ptah was the God of the North Pole, and that Knum, or Khnumn, or Khnumu, was the God of the South Pole, and that each of these divinities was associated with seven associate gods. In the case of Ptah these minor deities were said to have been his sons.

Our supposition is that since Ptah represents the pole of the heavens, his seven sons stand for seven successive positions of the pole brought about by precession. (George St. Clair, "Creation Records Discovered in Egypt," in *Studies in The Book of The Dead*, London: David Nutt, 1898, p. 103.)

As to the south polar god, we learn from the same authority that:

Khnumn was called Builder of Men, Maker of the Gods, the Father from the Beginning, Creator of Things which are, or shall be, etc. He supported the Heavens upon its four pillars, in the beginning; the earth, air, sea, and sky are his handiwork. Our idea is that Khnumn is the divinity of the South Pole, and contemporary with Ptah. The axis on which the universe turned had two pivots, and the southern god contributed to the work of creation as much as the northern god. We are told that Khnumn labored with Ptah in carrying out the work of creation ordered by Thoth; and again that Ptah was assisted in his work by the seven Khnumn, or architects. We remember the seven sons of Ptah. Ptah had modeled men with his own hands, and Khnumn had formed them on a potter's table. At Philae and at Denderah, Ptah is represented as piling upon his potter's table the plastic clay from which he is about to make a human body. Khnumn is sometimes represented as molding the egg of the Universe out of the matter furnished by Ptah. (St. Clair, *Creation Records*, p. 103.)

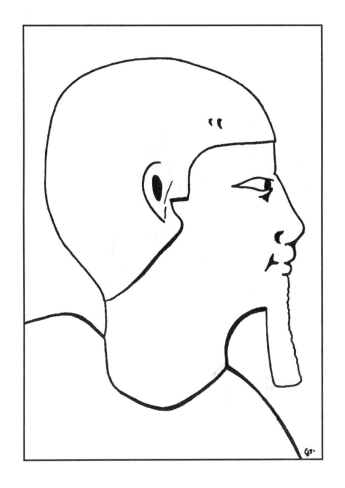

**Ptah**

**Khnum**

The Babylonians, according to Berossus [a priest of Bel at Babylon c. 250 B.C.), believed that the god Bel cut off his own head and that the other gods collected his blood and mixing it with earth, made men out of the paste; which explains why men are so wise; since their bodies are animated by the blood of a god. A similar tale was current in ancient Greece, where Prometheus created men and beasts out of clay.

> When he had done his work, some of the clay was left over, and might be seen on the spot long afterwards in the shape of two large boulders lying at the edge of a ravine. A Greek traveler, who visited the place in the second century of our era, thought that the boulders had the color of clay, and that they smelt strongly of human flesh. (Frazer, *Folklore*, p. 3.)

This act of creation by Prometheus was said to have occurred at Panopeus. "I too visited the spot some seventeen hundred and fifty years later," we are told by Frazer.

> It is a forlorn little glen, or rather hollow, on the southern side of the hill of Panopeus, below the long line of ruined but still stately walls and towers which crowns the gray rocks of the summit. It was a hot day in late autumn — the first of November — and after the long rainless summer of Greece the little glen was quite dry; no water trickled down its bushy sides, but in the bottom I found a reddish crumbling earth, perhaps a relic of the clay out of which Prometheus modeled our first parents. (Frazer, *Folklore*, p. 3.)

A creation myth of the Maoris of New Zealand records how the god, Tiki, mixed some of his own blood with red clay and modeled a man in his own image. The model was animated by the god breathing into his mouth and nose causing the effigy to come alive and sneeze. This first man was called *Tiki-Ahua* (Tiki's likeness).

In Tahiti, the first human couple were made by the god Taaroa. After creating the world, the god made the first man out of red earth. Then he put the man to sleep, and after extracting from him a bone *(ivi)*, fashioned it into a woman. This story was recorded for posterity by the missionary William Ellis, who declared that:

> This always appeared to me a mere recital of the Mosaic account of creation, which they had heard

from some European, and I never placed any reliance on it, although they have repeatedly told me it was a tradition among them before any foreigner arrived. Some have also stated that the woman's name was *Ivi*, which would be by them pronounced as if written Eve. *Ivi* is an aboriginal word, and not only signifies a bone, but also a widow, and a victim slain in war. Notwithstanding the assertion of the natives, I am disposed to think that *Ivi* or Eve is the only aboriginal part of the story, as far as it respects the mother of the human race. (William Ellis, *Polynesian Researches,* 2nd Ed., London: 1832-1836, i, 110 seq., cited in Frazer, *Folklore in The Old Testament,* Vol. I, London: Macmillan and Co., Ltd., p. 10.)

The opinion of the missionary was probably erroneous, for similar myths are current throughout Polynesia. In Bowditch Island there is a tradition that after the creator god made the first man, he then from earth produced the image of the woman, who immediately began to live. He then —

placed the happy pair in an earthly paradise, where, free from care and toil, they could live on the sweet fruits of a delightful garden, where birds and beasts frisked about them in fearless security. As a crowning mercy he planned for our first parents the great gift of immortality, but resolved to make them arbiters of their own fate by leaving them free to accept or reject the proffered boon. For that purpose he planted in the midst of the garden two wondrous trees that bore fruits of very different sorts, the fruit of the one being fraught with death to the eater, and the other with life eternal. Having done so, he sent the serpent to the man and woman and charged him to deliver this message: "Eat not of the Tree of Death, for in the day ye eat thereof ye shall surely die; but eat of the Tree of Life and live for ever." Now the serpent was more subtle than any beast of the field, and on his way he bethought him of changing the message; so, when he came to the, happy garden and found the woman alone in it, he said to her, "Thus saith God: Eat not of the Tree of Life, for in the day ye eat thereof ye shall surely die; but eat of the Tree of Death, and live for ever." The foolish woman believed him, and ate of the fatal fruit, and gave it to her husband, and he ate also. But the sly serpent himself ate of the Tree of Life. That is why men have been mortal and serpents immortal ever since, for serpents cast their skins every year and so renew their youth. If only the serpent had not perverted God's good message and deceived our first mother, we should have been immortal instead of the serpents; for like the serpents we should cast our skins every year and so renew our youth perpetually. (Frazer, *Folklore*, p. 19.)

The myths of the origin of death are based on two original stories: (1) the story of the Perverted Message, and (2) the story of the Cast Skin. Later mythologists combined the two original stories into the composite story of the Perverted Message and the Cast Skin. These myths seemed to have originated in Africa, but they were told all over the world in ancient times, and I shall cite a few examples.

A good example of the story of the Perverted Message survives among the Namaquas of South Africa. These people associate the phases of the moon with the idea of immortality. Once upon a time they say the moon wished to make mankind immortal, and the hare was entrusted with the message and was instructed to say: "As I die and rise to life again, so shall you die and rise to life again." The hare, either through forgetfulness or just plain carelessness, reversed the moons message, saying: "As I die and do not rise to life again, so shall you also die and not rise to life again." On learning of the hare's perversion of her message the moon hurled a stick at the animal which hitting him split his lip. This explains the cloven lip of the hare. A Namaqua elder stated that: "We are still enraged with the hare because he brought such a bad message, and we will not eat him." So, even to this day, when youths become of age among the Namaquas they are forbidden to partake of the flesh of a hare. A violation of this tabu may involve banishment from the community.

The Nandi of East Africa trace the origin of death to the ill-will of a certain dog. In the early ages of the world this dog appeared to a group of people and said: "All people will die like the Moon, but unlike the Moon you will not return to life again unless you give me some milk to drink out of your gourd and beer to drink through your straw. If you do this, I will arrange for you to go to the river when you die and to come to life again on the third day." The dog was laughed at by the people, who gave him milk and beer to drink off a stool. The dog resented not receiving the kind of service he requested and then said: "All people will die, and the Moon alone will return to life." This explains why when people die they stay dead, while the moon dies and then comes back to life after three days.

 "In this story," Frazer comments, "nothing is said as to the personage who sent the dog with the message of immortality to men; but from the messenger's reference to the Moon, and from a comparison with the parallel Hottentot story, we may reasonably infer that it was the Moon who employed the dog to run the errand, and that the unscrupulous animal misused his opportunity to extort privileges for himself to which he was not strictly entitled." (Frazer, *Folklore,* p. 21.)

 In some of the myths of the origin of death, two messengers are involved. For instance, there is a Hottentot story in which the couriers are an insect and a hare. The moon, it is said, told an insect to go to men and announce from the moon that: "As I die, and dying live, so ye shall also die, and dying live." The insect started on his errand but was halted by a hare. "On what errand are you bound," the hare asked. The insect replied: "I am sent by the Moon to men, to tell them that as she dies, and dying lives, they also shall die, and dying live." The hare then replied: "As you are an awkward runner, let me go." So the hare ran swiftly, while the insect followed at a leisurely pace. Coming to the men, the hare proclaimed he had a message from the moon, namely: "As I die, and dying perish, in the same manner you shall also die and come wholly to an end." The hare then went to the moon and told of how he had perverted her message. The moon angrily denounced the hare for his perfidy and whacked him on the nose with a stick, causing a slit in the nose, and this is why hares ever since have been afflicted with slit noses.

 The Masarwas, another South African people, tell a similar tale. In this case, the moon sent the tortoise with the glad tidings to men, but the tortoise dawdled along and kept repeating the message to himself so as not to forget it. This irked the moon, so she called the hare and said:

 "Since you are a swift runner, tell the men that as I, dying, live again, so they dying will live again." The hare also had a bad memory, so getting to the men announced the moon's message thusly: "As I dying live again, so you dying will die forever." The tortoise, following the hare, finally arrived and gave the right message, but, alas, he was too late. The men were angry at the hare for bringing them the wrong message, and as the hare sat nibbling grass, one of the men bounced a stone off the animal's mouth, splitting the upper lip. That is why hares have a cleft upper lip.

There are Ashanti versions of this myth in which the messengers were a sheep and a goat. According to these stories, in ancient days God visited his children and talked with them. On one occasion God looked on while some women were stirring a batch of mash in a mortar with pestles. This annoyed the women, and they told God to get lost; and meanwhile beat him with their pestles. So God went back to heaven and ceased visiting the world, but he bore no ill will to people. So one day he sent a goat to men with the message: "There is something which they call Death. He will kill some of you. But even if you die, you will not perish completely, you will come to me in Heaven." The goat started out to convey this intelligence but stopped on the way to browse on a bush. God looked down from heaven and noticed the loitering goat. A sheep was then dispatched with the same message and told to go without delay. The sheep, afflicted with amnesia, hurriedly arrived and told the people: "God sends you word that you will die, and that will be the end of you." The goat later arrived and gave the correct message, but the men replied: "No goat, that is not what God said. We believe that the message which the sheep brought us is the one which God sent to us." In another Ashanti version of this myth, the roles of the messengers are reversed; with the sheep setting out to bring the glad tidings of immortality to men. However, the goat overtook the sheep and got to men first and informed them they were mortal.

In the tales related above, the origin of death was ascribed to the error or deceit of one of the two messengers. There are, however, other versions current among the Bantus of Africa, in which God was responsible for man's loss of immortality. In these tales God is said to have decided to let death prevail. According to a Zulu myth, in the early days of the world Unkulunkulu (The Old Old One) sent a chameleon with a message to men: "Go, chameleon, go and say, 'Let not men die.'" The chameleon crawled along and stopped on the way to eat mulberries. The Old Old One sent the lizard with another message: "Lizard, when you have arrived, say 'Let men die.'" The lizard got there first and delivered his message. Then later the chameleon showed up and said: "It is said, 'Let not men die'." But the men replied: "We have heard the word of the lizard; we cannot hear your word. Through the word of the lizard, men will die."

The same, or a similar, story is told among other Bantus, such as the Basutos, Bechuanas, Baronga, and the Ngoni. The same tale in a slightly different form is current among the Hausas of West Africa.

We may conclude with Sir J. G. Frazer: "Thus the belief is widespread in Africa that God at one time purposed to make mankind immortal, but that the benevolent scheme miscarried through the fault of the messenger to whom he had entrusted the gospel message." (Frazer, *Folklore,* p. 26.)

The story of the Cast Skin is based on the belief that certain animals, particularly serpents, periodically cast their skins, and renewing their youth, do not die. Primitive men, who believed this, made up myths to explain why certain animals became immortal and why mankind remained mortal.

The Wabende and the Wafipa of East Africa tell of how the creator god, Leza, one day visited the world and said to all living creatures: "Who wishes not to die?" All other animals and man, except the serpent, were asleep, and they did not hear the question. The serpent, alone being awake, heard and replied: "I do." So that is why men and other animals die while the serpent crawls out of his old skin and, outfitted with a new skin, perpetually renews his youth. The serpent can only meet death by being killed. The Dusuns of North Borneo have preserved a similar tradition. The Creator, after making the world and all things in it, then announced: "Who is able to cast off his skin? If any one can do so, he shall not die." Only the snake heard this proclamation, and he promptly answered: "I can."

Similar beliefs were not unknown in the New World. The Arawaks of British Guiana told of how the creator came to earth to see how his human children were getting along. Men were so evil that they tried to kill the creator, so he rendered them mortal and gave eternal life to animals capable of casting their skins, such as beetles, lizards, and serpents. Another version of this myth has been preserved by the Tamanchiers of the Orinoco. The creator, after residing with them for some time, embarked on a boat to cross the ocean. On leaving the shore he announced: "You will change your skins," meaning: "You will renew your youth like beetles and snakes." An old woman hearing these words remarked sarcastically: "Oh." The creator, greatly annoyed, then said: "You shall die." And that of course is why mankind became mortal.

In the early ages of the world, life and death were believed to have some connection with the phases of the moon. This doctrine of lunar sympathy was subscribed to by the Mantras of the Malay Peninsula. Men in most ancient times did not die, but they grew thin as the moon wanes and became fat as the lunar orb waxes to full phase. This caused a population explosion since nobody was dying. A son of the first man called this fact to the attention of his father and asked him what should be done about it. The first man answered: "Leave things the way they are." A younger brother of the son of the first man dissented saying: "No, let men die like the banana, leaving their offspring behind." Finally, the question was submitted to the lord of the underworld who decided in favor of death. So men ceased renewing their youth like the moon and began to die like the banana. The inhabitants of the Caroline Islands believed that, in days of old, people died on the last day of the waning moon and came to life again at the appearance of the new moon, but an evil spirit intervened and arranged things so that once people were dead they remained in that condition. The Kaitish of Central Australia had a tradition that in the early days men were either buried underground or in trees, and that after three days they invariably arose from the dead. This congenial state of affairs was ended by the conduct of a man of the Curlew Totem, who, seeing two members of the Little Wallaby Totem engaged in burying a brother of the clan, proceeded to seize the corpse and kick it into the sea. Since that event nobody rose from the dead, and this is why nobody today rises from the dead after three days as everybody did in the days of the remote past. Nothing is said about the moon in the aforesaid story of the origin of death, but we may logically infer that the three days men of yore remained dead were the three days in which the light of the moon was invisible.

In many of these myths, pretending to account for the origin of death, the animal responsible for bringing death to mankind was the lizard. This is especially the case in many of the African traditions. In many African tales, Frazer noted:

> The instrument of bringing death among men is the lizard. We may conjecture that the reason for assigning the invidious office to a lizard was that this animal, like the serpent, casts its skin periodically, from which primitive man might infer, as he infers with regard to serpents, that the creature renews its youth and lives for ever. Thus all the myths which relate how a lizard or a serpent became the maleficent agent of human mortality may perhaps be referred to an old idea of a certain jealousy and rivalry between men and creatures which cast their skins, notably serpents and lizards; we may suppose that in all such cases, a story was told of a contest between man and his animal rivals for the possession of immortality, a contest in which, whether by mistake or guile, the victory always remained with the animals, who thus became immortal, while mankind was doomed to mortality. (Frazer, *Folklore,* p.31.)

We must now consider the composite story of the Perverted Message and the Cast Skin. Such a myth has been preserved by the

19

Gallas of East Africa. This tradition attempted to explain the immortality of serpents and the mortality of men. It seems that God sent a certain bird, dark blue or black in color, bearing a white mark on each wing and a crest on its head; this bird had been told to announce to men that when they had reached a state of senility they would cast their skins and thus renew their youth. The bird started out to deliver the glad tidings but on the way observed a snake eating carrion. The bird then said to the serpent that he would give him God's message if he, the snake, would share his meal with him. The snake said that he was not interested in hearing God's message, but the bird talked him around and the reptile was given the following message: "When men grow old they will die, but when you grow old you will cast your skin and renew your youth."

The story of the fall of man in the third chapter of Genesis seems to be an abridged edition of numerous primitive myths dealing with the origin of death. Frazer concluded that:

> Little is wanted to complete its resemblance to the similar myths still told by savages in many parts of the world. The principal, almost the only, omission is the silence of the narrator as to the eating of the fruit of the tree of life by the serpent, and the consequent attainment of immortality by the reptile. Nor is it difficult to account for the lacuna. The vein of rationalism, which runs through the Hebrew account of creation and has stripped it of many grotesque features that adorn or disfigure the corresponding Babylonian tradition, could hardly fail to find a stumbling block in the alleged immortality of serpents; and the redactor of the story in its final form has removed this stone of offense from the path of the faithful by the simple process of blotting out the incident entirely from the legend. Yet the yawning gap left by his sponge has not escaped the commentators, who look in vain for the part which should have been played in the narrative by the tree of life. If my interpretation of the story is right, it has been left for the comparative method, after thousands of years, to supply the blank in the ancient canvas, and to restore, in all their primitive crudity, the gay barbaric colors which the skillful hand of the Hebrew artist has softened or effaced. (Frazer, *Folklore*, pp. 32-33.)

All of the great nations of the ancient world had inherited creation myths similar to those recorded in the Bible from their primitive ancestors. I shall examine only a few representative examples, as concisely as possible.

## 1. *Egyptian*

(a) A god dwelling in a primeval abyss, where he had been since the beginning of time, uttered his own name, and by so doing caused himself to live.

(b) This god then created by magic a foundation on which to stand; probably the earth.

(c) From his mouth this god drew forth objects which reproduce themselves.

(d) He then created two other gods, male and female, who in turn propagated other gods.

(e) Next, vegetation and creeping things were created on the earth.

(f) Man was finally created from the tears falling from the eyes of the original god.

## 2. *Babylonian*

(a) There were primeval gods dwelling in an abyss.

(b) Other gods joined them later, and a conflict developed.

(c) Two of the primeval deities were slain. Another god, a female, created monsters and fought against the newly arrived gods, but was eventually killed.

(d) The new gods created the heavens and the earth from the body of the slain goddess.

(e) One of the gods was decapitated, and from his blood and bones, the first human beings were derived.

### 3. *Chinese*

(a) The world started as an atom formed from nothing.

(b) Over vast periods of time the original atom split in two, producing a male and a female principle. These also split in two, eventually into four elements.

(c) From the four elements a being was produced, whose body produced the constituents of the universe, and from whose decomposing corpse came worms, which eventually became human beings.

### 4. *Japanese*

(a) The world started from an atom, which produced male and female elements.

(b) These formed an egg, containing germs from which heaven and earth resulted.

(c) A species of reed-shoot grew up between heaven and earth and then changed into a god.

(d) Living beings were then born, and two of them united, giving birth to seas, rivers, islands, trees, herbs, and the various heavenly bodies.

### 5. *Celtic*

(a) The world was brought about by two principles; one creative, the other destructive.

(b) The destructive principle dwelled in an abyss.

(c) Life, in an atomic form, was created by the spoken words of the creative principle.

(d) Man originated in the abyss, then came to the earth.

## 6. Scandinavian

(a) In the beginning was a yawning abyss, bordered on one side by mist and cold and on the other side by fire.

(b) A spark from the fire melted some cold vapor, producing a giant.

(c) This giant then gave birth to a race of giants.

(d) The original giant had a cow which by licking a brine-covered rock produced the father of the gods.

(e) Other gods were engendered, and they in turn slew the giant and created the world from his body.

(f) The earth, covered with water, was lifted out of it by the gods.

(g) Finally, two figures were formed from trees, and were given life and understanding by the gods.

The myths and legends concerning the creation of the universe, of the world, and of man related in the Bible were widely believed by many educated people up to the beginning of the Age of Enlightenment in the eighteenth century. Since then evolution has triumphed, and science has superseded superstition to a considerable extent. With the rise of the science of Egyptology the biblical chronology of Ussher and Lightfoot was completely demolished. The ancient records of Egypt show that by the year 4004 B.C., supposedly the date of the beginning of the world, the Great Pyramid had already been built and had been used by the astronomers of Egypt as an observatory over long periods of time. Even before the rise of the culture of Egypt, there was the great Kushite, or Ethiopian civilization, which was widespread in both Africa and Asia. One of the greatest African Ethiopian temples was located at Abu Simbel, or Ipsambul, in Nubia. When an English traveler named Wilson visited this temple, he saw sculptured on its walls the story of the fall of man as told in Genesis. Adam and Eve were shown in the Garden of Eden as well as the tempting serpent and the fatal tree. Commenting on this fact, Godfrey Higgins asked: "How is the fact of the mythos of the second book of Genesis being found in Nubia, probably a thousand miles above Heliopolis, to be accounted for?" (Godfrey Higgins, *Anacalypsis*, Vol. I, London: Longmans, Green and Co., 1836, p. 403.) Higgins then added that: "The same mythos is found in India." For evidence he cited Colonel Tod's *History of Rajputana* as follows: "A drawing brought by Colonel Coombs, from a sculptured column in a cave-temple in the south of India represents the first pair at the foot of the ambrosial tree, and a serpent entwined among the heavily laden boughs, presenting to them some of the fruit from his mouth." (Higgins, *Anacalypsis*, Vol. I, pp. 403-404.) The ancient peoples of India were Asiatic Ethiopians and it should not surprise us that they shared common traditions with their brothers in Africa.

The scriptural record of the creation of the world confines it to the period of six days. Other ancient speculations were more liberal. The Indo-Persian system of Zoroaster, for instance, represented the creation as taking place over a time of 6,000 years. This chronology, as reproduced by Busenbark, is:

| 1st | 1,000 years | — Creation of the Sky |
| 2nd | 1,000 years | — Creation of the Water |
| 3rd | 1,000 years | — Creation of the Earth |
| 4th | 1,000 years | — Creation of the Planets |
| 5th | 1,000 years | — Creation of the Animals |
| 6th | 1,000 years | — Creation of Man |

(Busenbark, *Symbols*, p. 297.)

The stories in Genesis tell of a flat earth, which was apparently the center of the universe, with the world stationary, and the sun moving around it. The priests of ancient Egypt would have laughed at this crude cosmogony, for they had much more advanced knowledge in this field. An ancient Egyptian account of the origin of the world has been translated by Dr. Churchward as follows:

> Then God . . . sent forth his edict to each one of the suns and commanded them to emit worlds, and every sun that was in the universe sent forth from his bosom a choir of planets. Thus began the solar system that exists, each sun being the center of the planets which he evolved, and every planet revolving about that center, from whose glowing bosom he had birth. Many and various were the planets evolved according to the nature of the suns from which they came, according also the manifold existences which God foresaw would be produced thenceforth. When the

planets were evolved *from* the sun, they were sent forth at first in gaseous vapor, immense revolving spheres projected into space, but bound by laws in the parent star. When this vapor subsided and condensed, they became mighty spheres of water, whirling along their regulated paths. When ages and ages rolled into the gulfs of ages and ages, and ages and ages vanished into the abyss of time, the sphere became solidified with earthly particles and ceased to be a watery globe; and thus, as years revolved on years, and the forces of nature exercised their powers, and heat contended with cold, and vapor with solid; there were volcanic changes and fiery revolutions, and many deluges. Then the earth gradually assumed its present shape, having been the grave of successive generations, until the race that now exists upon it assumed unto themselves living developments. Dr. Albert Churchward *(The Signs and Symbols of Primordial Man,* London: George Allen and Co., 1913, pp. 335-336.)

The advanced mathematical and astronomical knowledge possessed by the Egyptian scientists in the Pyramid Age, more than 6,000 years ago, has been largely ignored by contemporary scholars, so I shall touch upon it briefly.

A good summary of some of this suppressed knowledge has been given by Professor Stecchini in the following passage:

Information about the Egyptian estimate of the size and shape of the earth is provided by Chapter LXIV of the *Book of the Dead.* In one of the papyri of the *Book of the Dead* there is an annotation to the effect that this chapter was found in the shrine of the solar boat during the reign of Udimu, the fourth or fifth pharaoh of the First Dynasty. Chapter LXIV states that the spirits of the Nether World, (that is all that is below the surface of the earth) are 4,601,200 and that each is 12 cubits high. The occurrence of the factor 12 indicates that is a matter of geographic cubits. Now 12 x 4,601,200 cubits = 55,214,000 cubits = 138,036 geographic stadia, is equal to two diameters of the earth. In order to explain the figure 138,036 stadia, one must assume that the Egyptians reckoned as if the polar flattening occurs only in the northern hemisphere. On the basis of this assumption, the figure of 138,036 stadia can be decomposed into the following earth radii:

34,538 stadia=6,378,388 meters=Equatorial Radius
34,538 stadia
34,538 stadia
34,422 stadia=6,356,966 meters=Polar Radius
138,036 stadia

These figures imply that the flattening of the North Pole is 116/34,538 = 1/297.74. With extreme economy of numerical expression, the Egyptians had arrived at values which are as good as the best modern ones. (Peter Tompkins, *Secrets of The Great Pyramid,* with an Appendix by Livio Catullo Stecchini, New York: Harper and Row, 1971, p. 369.)

I believe that a summary of the evidence adduced by modern science relating to the origin of the world; the story of cosmic, organic, and social evolution, and of man and his works should be of value to the reader, and this information is tabulated below.

### *Evolution: — A Summary*

Origin of the World . . . . . . 10,000,000,000 Years Ago

Origin of Life . . . . . . . . . . . . .2,000,000,000 Years Ago

1st Vertebrates (Fish) . . . . . . .400,000,000 Years Ago

Amphibians . . . . . . . . . . . . . . 300,000,000 Years Ago

Reptiles . . . . . . . . . . . . . . . . .270,000,000 Years Ago

Birds & Mammals . . . . . . . . . .150,000,000 Years Ago

Apes . . . . . . . . . . . . . . . . . . . . .40,000,000 Years Ago

Man branched off from ape ancestors in Africa about 25,000,000 years ago.

First true men appeared in Africa from 2,500,000 to 5,000,000 years ago.

First civilization in Africa at least 20,000 years ago.

Among the early civilizations were those of the Pygmies, Ethiopians, Egyptians, Mesopotamians, Minoans, Dravidians, Olmecs, Mayans, Aztecs, Incans, Mound Builders, etc.

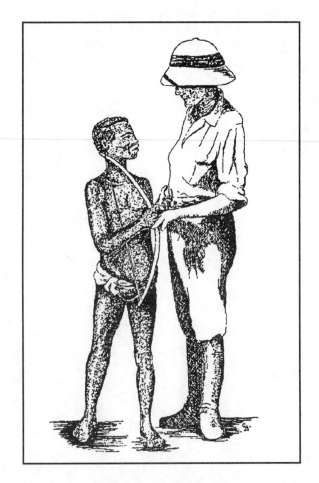

**Pygmy tribesman**

# Chapter II
# The Great Deluge

We are all familiar with the story of the Flood as given in Holy Writ. We recall that the first man and woman were created in a state of perfection, but that they soon fell from grace and were expelled from Eden. Mankind went downward rapidly. The first murder occurred in the first family, when Cain slew Abel. We are told that Cain fled to the Land of Nod and took unto himself a wife. This story has been embarrassing to true believers, for according to Scripture, Adam and Eve and their two sons were the only people in the world at that time. As mankind waxed in wickedness the good Lord finally decided to take steps through the proper channels, and here is the story as given in the sacred anthology:

> And God saw that the wickedness of man was great in the earth, and that every imagination of the thoughts of his heart was only evil continually. And it repented the Lord that he had made man on the earth, and it grieved him at his heart.
>
> And the Lord said, I will destroy man whom I have created from the face of the earth; both man and beast, and the creeping things, and the fowls of the air; for it repenteth me that I have made them. But Noah found grace in the eyes of the Lord . . . and God said unto Noah, the end of all flesh is come before me, for the earth is filled with violence through them, and behold, I will destroy them with the earth. Make thee an ark of gopher wood, rooms shalt thou make in the ark, a window shalt thou make in the ark; . . . And behold, I, even I, do bring a flood of waters upon the earth, to destroy all flesh, wherein is the breath of life, from under heaven, and every thing that is in the earth shall die. But with thee shall I establish my covenant; and thou shalt come into the ark, thou and thy sons, and thy wife, and thy sons' wives, with thee. And of every living thing of all flesh, two of every sort shalt thou bring into the ark, to keep them alive with thee; they shall be male and female. Of fowls after their kind, and of cattle after their kind, of every creeping thing of the earth after his kind, two of every

Cain and Abel

sort shall come in to thee, to keep them alive. And take thou unto thee of all food that is eaten and thou shall gather it to thee; and it shall be for food for thee and for them. Thus did Noah, according to all that God had commanded him.

The passage cited above is from the sixth chapter of Genesis. In Genesis 7:1-3, we read that after the ark had been completed, the Lord said to Noah: "Come thou and all thy house into the ark... of every clean beast thou shall take to thee by sevens, the male and his female; and of beasts that are not clean by two, the male and his female. Of fowls also of the air by sevens, and the male and his female." Then we read: "Noah went in, and his sons, and his wife, and his sons' wives with him, into the ark."

Thereafter began the Great Flood. A rain of forty days and forty nights covered the entire earth. As the waters subsided the ark is said to have landed on top of Mt. Ararat. Before landing his craft, Noah had sent out birds to search for land, a raven and a dove. The dove finally came back with an olive leaf, giving proof that the land was now above the water. After Noah and his crew had disembarked from the ark, we read: "And Noah builded an altar unto the Lord, . . . and offered burnt offerings on the altar. And the Lord smelled a sweet savor, and the Lord said in his heart, I will not again curse the ground anymore for man's sake." (Genesis 8.)

The myths concerning a great deluge are quite numerous. Frazer devotes over one hundred pages to them in his great study of the Old Testament folklore. Here I have space for only a brief discussion of parallel examples from the ancient mythos.

The Chaldean account of the great flood as recorded by Berossus reads as follows:

> After the death of Ardates (the ninth king of the Chaldeans) his son Xisuthrus reigned eighteen sari. In his time happened a great deluge, the history of which is thus described: The deity Kronos appeared to him in a vision and warned him that upon the fifteenth day of the month Daesius there would be a flood, by which mankind would be destroyed. He therefore enjoined him . . . to build a vessel, and take with him into it his friends and relations, and to convey on board everything necessary to sustain life,

together with all the different animals, both birds and quadrupeds, and trust himself fearlessly to the deep. He then obeyed the divine admonition, and built a vessel five stadia in length, and two in breadth. Into this he put everything which he had prepared, and last of all conveyed into it, his wife, his children, and his friends. After the flood had been upon the earth, and was in time abated, Xisuthrus sent out birds from the vessel; which not finding any food, nor any place whereupon they might rest their feet, returned to him again. After an interval of some days, he sent them forth a second time; and they now returned, with their feet tinged with mud. He made a trial a third time with these birds; but they returned to him no more; from whence he judged that the surface of the earth had appeared above the waters. He therefore made an opening in the vessel, and upon looking out, found that it was stranded upon the side of some mountain; upon which he immediately quitted it, with his wife, his daughter and the pilot. Xisuthrus then paid his adoration to the earth, and having constructed an altar, offered sacrifices to the gods.

The account just cited (George Smith, *The Chaldean History of Berossus,* New York: Scribner Armstrong and Co., 1876, pp. 285-286) not only closely agrees with the Genesis story, but also with that excavated from earlier Assyrian archives by George Smith of the British Museum. "When we consider," Smith wrote, "the difference between the two countries of Palestine and Babylonia, these variations do not appear greater than we should expect . . . Thus we should expect beforehand that there would be differences in the narrative, and such we usually find, and we may also notice that the uniform account does not always coincide even with the account of the same events given by Berossus from Chaldean sources.

The Babylonian and Biblical deluge myths are so similar that they must have been derived from some more ancient common source. In both instances a god warns a virtuous man of the coming of a flood. The man is instructed to build an ark, and take into it people, animals, etc. In both cases after the flood, birds are sent out three times from the ark. The ark in both stories landed on a mountain. After leaving the ark, the survivors offered up a sacrifice to the gods. Xisuthrus was the tenth king and Noah was the tenth patriarch. The three sons of Xisuthrus were Titan, Zerovanos and

Japetosthes. The three sons of Noah were Ham, Shem and Japheth.

The Biblical story of the flood has an appendix which has had tragic historical consequences. It was related that in celebrating the end of the flood, Noah imbibed too much of an alcoholic beverage, bringing on a drunken state which caused the patriarch to take off all his clothes and to dance around in a state of nudity. One son, Ham, witnessing this orgy, thought it was funny, and laughed at it. This conduct, according to the Bible, called forth a divine curse. Ham was turned black by the good Lord, and exiled to Africa, and he and his children were doomed to hew wood and draw water for their more fortunate brothers. This propaganda was used to justify the slave trade and is still regarded as gospel truth by Christian racists.

There are several Hindu versions of the myth of a great deluge, the oldest being that published in the *Satapatha Brahmana,* about the sixth century B.C.

The following condensed account is taken from an authoritative version:

> Many ages after the creation of the world, Brahma resolved to destroy it with a deluge, on account of the wickedness of the people. There lived at the time a pious man named Satyavrata, and as the Lord of the Universe loved this pious man and wished to preserve him from the sea of destruction which was to appear on account of the depravity of the age, he appeared before him in the form of Vishnu (the Preserver) and said: "In seven days from the present time . . . the world will be plunged in an ocean of death but in the midst of the destroying waves, a large vessel sent by me for thy use shall stand before thee. Then shalt thou take all medicinal herbs, all the variety of foods, and accompanied by seven saints, encircled by pairs of all brute animals, thou shalt enter the spacious ark, and continue in it, secure from the flood, on an immense ocean, without light, except the light of thy holy companions. When the ship shall be agitated by an impetuous wind, thou shall fasten it with a large sea serpent on my horn; for I will be near thee (in the form of a fish) drawing the vessel with thee and thy attendants." (Thomas William Doane, *Bible Myths*

*and Their Parallels in Other Religions,* New Hyde
Park, New York: University Books, 1970, p. 24.)

Read as mythology, the various stories of a great deluge have
considerable cultural value, but taken as history, they are asinine
and absurd. This viewpoint was eloquently expressed by Colonel
Robert G . Ingersoll in his inimitable style:

> We read the pagan sacred books with profit and
> delight. With myth and fable we are ever charmed,
> and find a pleasure in the endless repetition of the
> beautiful, poetic, and absurd. We find in all these
> records of the past, philosophies and dreams, and
> efforts stained with tears, of great and tender souls
> who tried to pierce the mystery of life and death, to
> answer the eternal questions of whence and whither,
> and vainly sought to make with bits of shattered glass
> a mirror, that would, in very truth, reflect the face and
> form of nature's perfect self.
>
> These myths were born of hopes, and fears, and
> tears, and smiles, and they were touched and colored
> by all there is of joy and grief between the rosy dawn
> of birth and death's sad night. They clothed even the
> stars with passion and gave to gods the faults and
> frailties of the sons of men. In them the winds and
> waves were music, and all the lakes, and streams and
> springs, the mountains, woods, and perfumed dells
> were haunted by a thousand fairy forms. They
> thrilled the veins of Spring with tremulous desire;
> made tawny Summer's billowed breast the throne and
> home of love; filled Autumn's arms with sun-kissed
> grapes and gathered sheaves; and pictured Winter as
> a weak old king who felt, like Lear upon his withered
> face, Cordelia's tears. These myths, though false, are
> beautiful, and have for many ages and in countless
> ways enriched the heart and kindled thought. But if
> the world were taught that all these things are true,
> and all inspired of God, and that eternal punishment
> will be the lot of him who dares deny or doubt, the
> sweetest myth of all the Fable World would lose its
> beauty and become a scorned and hateful thing to
> every brave and thoughtful man. (Robert G. Ingersoll,
> *Selected Lectures,* New York: Willey Book Co., 1938,
> pp. 9-10.)

Further on in this same work, Colonel Bob illustrated these views by submitting the Bible flood story to the scrutiny of reason. Ingersoll lectured and wrote with great charm, and the following extracts are given in his own words:

We know that there are many animals on this continent not found in the Old World. These must have been carried from here to the ark, and then brought back afterwards. Were the peccary, armadillo, anteater, sloth, agouti, vampire bat, marmoset, howling and prehensile-tailed monkey, the raccoon and muskrat carried by the angels from America to Asia? How did they get there? Did the polar bear leave his field of ice and journey toward the tropics? How did he know where the ark was? Did the kangaroo swim or jump from Australia to Asia? Did the giraffe, hipopotamus, antelope and orangutan journey from Africa in search of the ark? Can absurdities go further than this?

What had these animals to eat while on the journey? What did they eat while on the ark? What did they drink? When the rain came, of course the rivers ran to the seas, and these seas rose and finally covered the world. The waters of the seas mingled with those of the flood would make all salt. It has been calculated that it required to drown the world about eight times as much water as was in all the seas. To find how salty the waters of the flood must have been, take eight quarts of fresh water and add one quart from the sea. Such water would create instead of allay thirst. Noah had to take in his ark fresh water for all his beasts, birds and living things. He had to take the proper food for all. How long was he in the ark? Three hundred and seventy-seven days! Think of the food necessary for the monsters of the antediluvian world! Eight persons did all the work. They attended to the wants of 175,000 birds, 3,616 beasts, 1,300 reptiles, and 2,000,000 insects, saying nothing of the countless animalculae. Well after they all got in Noah pulled down the window, God shut the door and the rain commenced.

How long did it rain?
Forty days.

How deep did the water get?

About five and and half miles.

How much did it rain a day?

Enough to cover the whole world to a depth of about seven hundred and forty-two feet . . .

How many trees can live under miles of water for a year? What became of the soil, mashed, scattered, dissolved, and covered with the debris of a world? How were the tender plants and herbs preserved? How were the animals preserved after leaving the ark? There was no grass except such as had been submerged for a year. There were no animals to be devoured by the carnivorous beasts. What became of the birds that devoured other birds?

It must be remembered that the pressure of the water when at the highest point, say twenty-nine thousand feet, would have been about eight hundred tons on each square foot. Such a pressure certainly would have destroyed nearly every vestige of vegetable life, so that when the animals came out of the ark, there was not a mouthful of food in the wide world. How were they supported until the world was again clothed with grass? How were those animals taken care of that subsisted on others? Where did the bees get honey and the ants seeds? There was not a creeping thing on the whole earth; not a breathing creature beneath the whole heavens; not a living substance. Where did the tenants of the ark get food? There is but one answer if the story is true. The food necessary, not only during the year of the flood, but sufficient for many months afterwards, must have been stored in the ark. There is probably not an animal in the world that will not in a year eat and drink ten times its weight. Noah must have provided food and water for a year while in the ark and food for at least six months after they got on shore. It must have required for a pair of elephants about one hundred and fifty tons of food and water. A couple of mammoths would have required about twice that amount. Of course, there were other monsters that lived on trees and in a year would have devoured quite a forest. How would eight persons have distributed this food, even if the ark had been large enough to hold it?

How was the ark kept clean?

How did the animals get back to their respective countries? Some had to creep back about six thousand miles, and they could only go a few feet a day. Some of the creeping things must have started for the ark just as soon as they were made and kept up a steady jog for sixteen hundred years. Think of a couple of the slowest snails leaving a point opposite the ark and starting for the plains of Shinar, a distance of twelve thousand miles. Going at the rate of a mile a month, it would take them a thousand years. How did they get there? Polar bears must have come several thousand miles, and so sudden a change of climate must have been exceedingly trying upon their health. How did they know the way to go? Of course, all the polar bears did not go. Only two were required. Who selected these? Two sloths had to make the journey from South America. These creatures cannot travel to exceed three rods a day. [1 rod = 16 1/2 feet —ed.] At this rate they would make a mile in about a hundred days. They must have gone about six thousand miles to reach the ark. Supposing them to have traveled by a reasonably direct route, in order to complete the journey before Noah hauled in the plank, they must have started several years before the world was created. We must also consider that these sloths had to board themselves on the way, and that most of their time had to be taken up getting food and water. It is exceedingly doubtful whether a sloth could travel six thousand miles and board himself in less than three thousand years.

Volumes might be written upon the infinite absurdity of this most incredible wicked and foolish of all the fables contained in the last repository of the impossible called the Bible. To me it is a matter of amazement that it ever was for a moment believed by any intelligent human being. (Ingersoll, *Selected Lectures,* pp. 149-155.)

There are some students of mythology who regard all of the deluge stories as having a common origin, and originally, they had nothing to do with water, but were related to the sun, the moon and the stars. This was the conclusion arrived at by Ingersoll, who said:

I believe, though, that the real origin of all these myths is the same, and that it was originally an effort to account for the sun and moon and stars. The sun and moon were the man and wife, or the god and goddess, and the stars were their children. From a celestial myth it became a terrestrial one; the air or ether-ocean became a flood, produced by rain and the sun, moon and stars became man and woman and children. In the original story, the mountain was the place where in the far east the sky was supposed to touch the earth and it was there that the ship containing the celestial passengers finally rested from its voyage. (Ingersoll, *Selected Lectures,* p. 168.)

The astronomical origin of the deluge myths are discussed at length in Gerald Massey *(The Natural Genesis,* London: Williams and Norgate, 1883; reissued, New York: Weiser, 1974) and in George St. Clair *(Creation Records),* and last, but not least, in Godfrey Higgins *(Anacalypsis).*

Orthodox Christians, since they are committed to a belief in the literal truth of the Bible, hold that after the flood men became even more evil than they were before, so that 4,000 years after the creation of the world, god sent his only begotten son to suffer and die for the salvation of the human race. This ministry of Jesus, the Christ, was supposed to be a unique event in human history. This opinion is no longer tenable among those who accept reason as the criterion of truth. We know that St. Augustine believed that Christianity antedated the Christian era. We now know that many Saviors antedated the Christian era. A book was published in 1875 by Kersey Graves *(The World's Sixteen Crucified Saviors: or Christianity Before Christ,* New Hyde Park, NY: University Books, 1971). Early in the present century a scholarly Christian clergyman, the Reverend Charles H. Vail, wrote a book with the title *The World's Saviors.* In that work he gave the names of about twenty-five Pre-Christian, virgin-born, Savior-Gods, along with the stories of their lives. There is now an extensive literature on the various Savior-Gods. Most of these books have been written by scholars for scholars. The rest of the essay will be an attempt to popularize this material so as to make it comprehensible to the intelligent general reader, who does not have an extensive knowledge of comparative religion.

# Chapter III
# The Savior God Cults

Comparative hierologists have discovered records of about thirty Savior-God religions. These cults spread over all the world in very remote times, but they show evidence of a common origin. The various Savior-Gods had the following similar traits:

(1) They were born on or near Christmas.
(2) Their mothers were virgins.
(3) They were born in a cave or stable.
(4) They worked for the salvation of humanity.
(5) They were called Saviors, Mediators, Healers, etc.
(6) They were overcome by evil powers.
(7) A descent into Hell was made by them.
(8) After being slain they arose from death and
   ascended to heaven at Easter.
(9) They founded religious institutions.
(10) They were commemorated by Eucharistic rites.
(11) Many of these Savior-Gods were believed to make
   a second coming to the world.

The symbolism of the savior-god cults has been well summarized by Arthur Findlay whom we are pleased to cite:

> The belief in the return of Christ, which has prevailed throughout the Christian era, is just the descendant of this old belief that the Savior-God would return to earth . . . This return of the Savior was associated by the Babylonians and Egyptians in relation to the sun . . . They mapped out an imaginary zone in the heavens, within which lay the paths of the sun, moon and principal planets. It was divided into twelve signs, marked by twelve constellations called the Zodiac, and there was a ceremony or feast to celebrate the entrance of the sun into each sign. The ancients regarded the various heavenly bodies as visible expressions of divine intelligence, and the twelve constellations were considered to be the sun's bodyguard, this number being given to the Savior-God-man as the number of his disciples.

| | | |
|---|---|---|
| ♈ ARIES RAM | ♉ TAURUS BULL | ♊ GEMINI TWINS |
| ♋ CANCER CRAB | ♌ LEO LION | ♍ VIRGO MAID |
| ♎ LIBRA BALANCE | ♏ SCORPIO SCORPION | ♐ SAGITTARIUS ARCHER |
| ♑ CAPRICORNUS GOAT | ♒ AQUARIUS WATER·BEARER | ♓ PISCES FISHES |

**The Zodiac Constellations**

The word "Christ" means the anointed one . . . thus the Savior-God worshippers looked upon their savior as the Christ, which word has come down to us from the Greek word *Christos*, meaning "the anointed." A similar word was also used for these saviors, meaning good, excellent, beneficent, and gracious. The word the Greeks used was *Chrestos*; and we find these two words, *Christos* and *Chrestos* in use prior to the Christian era.

Of all the countries surrounding the Mediterranean in those days, the Jews alone were without a Savior-God, and their comfort came from their anticipation of his coming to earth and reigning over them as god-man. This idea was not peculiar to the Jews as, at least fifteen hundred years before the Hebrews thought of a Messiah, the Egyptians were writing of the coming just ruler who would lead the people on the road to righteousness . . . the Jews evidently borrowed the belief from Egypt, and called this anticipated righteous leader by the name of Messiah, which conveyed to them the same idea as Christos did to the Greeks. He was the expected anointed Jewish King, who was to subdue all their enemies, whereas the Christ of the Greeks, and the neighboring nations, was the anointed victim who had suffered on the altar as a sacrifice for their sins. (Arthur Findlay, *The Psychic Stream*, London: Psychic Press, 1947, pp. 209-211.)

Of all the numerous savior-gods, Findlay, in the work cited above, discussed at length the following divinities:

(1) Bel of Babylonia
(2) Osiris of Egypt
(3) Prometheus of Greece
(4) Mithra of Persia
(5) Krishna of India

I shall avail myself of some of the scholarly results of Arthur Findlay's research to which will be added valuable data from other sources and authorities.

**Baal (Bel)**

# Chapter IV
# Bel: The Babylonian Christ

In the British Museum there is an ancient tablet from Babylon, dating back to about 2000 B.C. This document is a description of a passion play relating to the god Bel. (The same divinity was called Baal among the ancient Hebrews.) This dramatic performance consisted often acts, or scenes, which we now briefly summarize:

**ACT 1: *Bel is taken prisoner.***

> Among the actors of the drama, the one representing Bel was arrested by soldiers, and taken off the stage.

**ACT 2: *Bel is tried in the Hall of Justice.***

> Here we have a trial in a courtroom. There was a judge and witnesses who gave testimony for and against the victim, who, though found innocent, was sentenced to death.

**ACT 3: *Bel is smitten.***

> Bel was in this scene abused and jeered at by the mob. As the prophet Isaiah later worded it: "He is despised and rejected of men; a man of sorrows, and acquainted with grief: and we hid as it were *our* faces from him; he was despised, and we esteemed him not."

**ACT 4: *Bel is led away to the Mount.***

> The actor representing Bel was taken under guard to a hilltop on which was a sacred grove.

**ACT 5: *With Bel are taken two malefactors, one of whom is released.***

In this scene two criminals were tried. One was found guilty and the other innocent. The guilty malefactor was sentenced to death, and the innocent one was released. The death of the god was not enacted in the amphitheater. "This may be," said Findlay, "because it took place on a hill where he was hung on one of the trees in the sacred grove, or crucified or slain on an altar, and so could not be enacted on the stage. By now the theater is empty and everyone has climbed to the top of the hill to witness the death scene ...after the death scene the people return to the amphitheater." (Findlay, *Psychic Stream,* p. 227.)

## ACT 6: *After Bel has gone to the mount, the city breaks into tumult.*

In this scene a mob appeared on the stage depicting the tumult resulting from the death of Bel.

## ACT 7: *Bel's clothes are carried away.*

The corpse of Bel, returned from the Mount, was stripped of its clothing and prepared for burial.

## ACT 8: *Bel goes down into the Mount and disappears from life.*

On the side of the hill near the stage was a tomb into which the body of Bel was interred.

## ACT 9: *Weeping women seek Bel at the Tomb.*

This scene has been well explained by Findlay as follows: "The beliefs surrounding Bel included the belief that he was seen after death in his etheric body. Quite possibly he was seen first of all by a woman, as women are today, and always have been, more clairvoyant than men . . . Then comes the final scene, depicting what all this display has been leading up to." (Findlay, *Psychic Stream,* pp. 229-230.)

## ACT 10: *Bel is brought back to life.*

A stone had sealed up the tomb of Bel. In this final scene of the drama, the stone was roiled away, and Bel walked out of the tomb in funeral garb. As Findlay has stated: "As he emerges from the tomb the audience rises and shouts in its frenzy till all are hoarse. The great drama has reached its climax. Their god has reappeared to prove to them that death has been conquered, and that he has secured for all, life in the hereafter . . . This great religious service has never been forgotten. It was copied by the Greeks, and is still performed in memory of Christ." (Findlay, *Psychic Stream*, p. 230.)

The parallels between the Babylonian and Christian myths are so similar that they have been tabulated by George R. Goodman in an article: "Easter" in *The Freethinker,* May 14, 1965:

| *Babylonian Legend* | *Christian Legend* |
| --- | --- |
| Bel is taken prisoner. | Jesus is taken prisoner. |
| Bel is tried in the Hall of Justice. | Jesus is tried in the Hall of Justice. |
| Bel is smitten | Jesus is scourged. |
| Bel is led away to the mount. | Jesus is led away to Golgotha. |
| With Bel are taken two malefactors; one of whom is released | With Jesus two malefactors are led away; another, Barabbas, is released. |
| After Bel has gone to the Mount the city breaks out in tumult. | At the death of Jesus the veil of the Temple is rent; the dead come from the graves and enter the city. |
| Bel's clothes are carried away. | Jesus' robe is divided among the soldiers. |

| | |
|---|---|
| Bel goes down into the Mount and disappears from life, | Jesus, from the grave, goes down into the realm of the dead. |
| A weeping woman seeks him at the gate of burial, | Mary Magdalene comes weeping to the tomb to seek Jesus. |
| Bel is brought back to life. | Jesus rises from the grave alive. |

This chapter on Bel, the Babylonian Christ, is based on a tablet discovered in the ruins of Babylon by Professor H. Zimmern. The Curator of the Babylonian Section of the British Museum supplied Arthur Findlay with a translation of this document. This material was discussed by Mr. Findlay in his book, *The Psychic Stream,* and for further details the reader is referred to that work. Findlay is an authority on psychical research. He was a founder, and for awhile, Chairman of the International Institute of Psychical Research; and was also Vice-President of the Glasgow Society of Psychical Research and the Leicester Society for Psychical Research.

# Chapter V
# Adonis of Syria and Attis of Phrygia

The worship of Adonis was quite popular among the Semites of Western Asia around 2000 B.C., and the Greeks borrowed it from them about the seventh century B.C. The actual name of this god was Tammuz, since Adonis, the Semitic *Adon,* is a title meaning "Lord." The Greeks through error converted this title of honor into a proper name. The Adonis cult was of pre-Semitic origin going back to the Sumerians, the earliest civilized peoples of Mesopotamia. This fact has been concisely expressed by Frazer:

> While Tammuz or his equivalent Adonis enjoyed a wide and lasting popularity among peoples of the Semitic stock, there are grounds for thinking that his worship originated with a race of other blood and other speech, the Sumerians, who in the dawn of history inhabited the flat alluvial plain at the head of the Persian Gulf and created the civilization which was afterwards called Babylonia. . . . In Southern Babylonia the Sumerians attained at a very early period to a considerable pitch of civilization; for they tilled the soil, reared cattle, built cities, dug canals, and even invented a system of writing, which their Semitic neighbors in time borrowed from them. (Sir James Frazer, *Adonis, Attis, Osiris,* Vol. I, New Hyde Park, New York: University Books, 1961. p. 7.)

Tammuz, or Adonis, was one of the oldest gods of the Sumerian pantheon. In the Babylonian mythology Adonis is regarded as the youthful consort and lover of Ishtar, the great mother goddess. He was believed to die annually and to descend to the underworld. His divine mistress would then journey to hell to bring him back to earth. During the sojourn of Ishtar in the infernal regions, love was banished from the world and the reproduction of life came to a halt. The great god Ea found it necessary to send a messenger to Allatu, queen of the infernal regions, demanding the return of Adonis and Ishtar to the upper world, so that the life cycle should continue to operate according to the laws of nature. In more than one

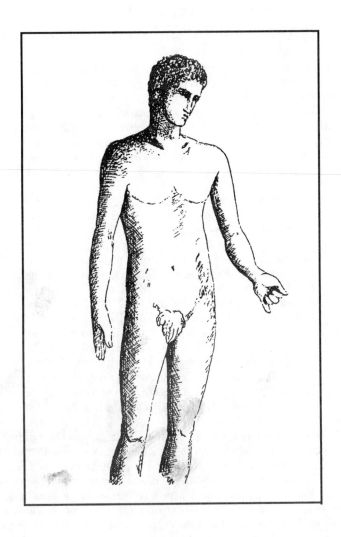

**Adonis**

**Tammuz**

Babylonian hymn Tammuz is likened to plants that rapidly fade away. One such lament reads:

A tamarisk that in the garden has drunk no water,
  whose crown in the field has brought forth no blossom,
A willow that rejoiced not by the watercourse,
A willow whose roots were torn up,
A herb that in the garden had drunk no water.

The death of this deity was annually mourned during the midsummer month of Tammuz by his devotees, who chanted dirges over his effigy to the accompaniment of the music of flutes. The laments were chanted over an effigy of the dead god, which was bathed with water, anointed with oil and clothed in a crimson robe, while the fumes of incense brought the dead deity back to life. The Greeks later on adopted and adapted this theme to their own mythology. The Greek version was restated by Frazer with characteristic charm:

> The tragical story and the melancholy rites of Adonis are better known to us from the descriptions of Greek writers than from the fragments of Babylonian literature or the brief reference of the prophet Ezekiel, who saw the women of Jerusalem weeping for Tammuz at the north gate of the temple. Mirrored in the glass of Greek mythology, the oriental deity appears as a comely youth beloved by Aphrodite. In his infancy the goddess hid him in a chest, which she gave in charge to Persephone, queen of the nether world. But when Persephone opened the chest and beheld the beauty of the babe, she refused to give him back to Aphrodite, though the goddess of love went down herself to hell to ransom her dear one from the power of the grave. The dispute between the two goddesses of love and death was settled by Zeus, who decreed that Adonis should abide with Persephone in the underworld for one part of the year, and with Aphrodite in the upper world for another part. At last the fair youth was killed in hunting by a wild boar, or by the jealous Ares, who turned himself into the likeness of a boar in order to compass the death of his rival. Bitterly did Aphrodite lament the loved and lost Adonis. The strife between the divine rivals for the possession of Adonis appears to be depicted on an Etruscan mirror. The two goddesses, identified by

**Ishtar**

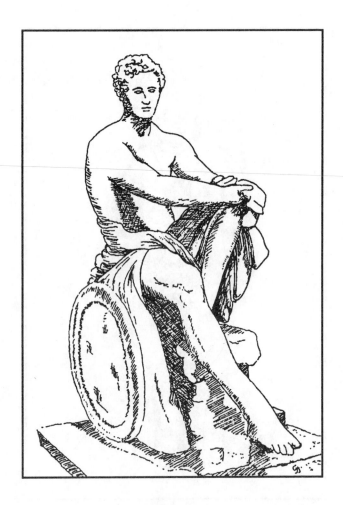

**Ares**

**Jupiter**

inscriptions, are stationed on either side of Jupiter, who occupies the seat of judgment and lifts an admonitory finger as he looks sternly towards Persephone. Overcome with grief the goddess of love buries her face in her mantle, while her pertinacious rival, grasping a branch in one hand, points with the other at a closed coffer, which probably contains the youthful Adonis. In this form of the myth, the contest between Aphrodite and Persephone for the possession of Adonis clearly reflects the struggle between Ishtar and Allatu in the land of the dead, while the decision of Zeus that Adonis is to spend one part of the year underground and another part above ground is merely a Greek version of the annual disappearance and reappearance of Tammuz. (Frazer, *Adonis, Attis, Osiris,* Vol. I, pp. 10-12.)

The myth of Adonis was localized and his rites solemnly practiced at two cities in Western Asia. These places were Byblus, on the Syrian coast, and Paphos in Cyprus. Now both of these cities were seats of the worship of Astarte or Ishtar, and according to tradition, both were ruled by King Cinyras, the father of Adonis. Byblus was the older of the two cities. It was said to have been founded in the dim and distant past by the great god El, whom the Greeks called Kronus and the Romans Saturn. In early historical times Byblus was the religious capital of the nation. To the Phoenicians it was what Jerusalem was to the Jews and Mecca to the Moslems in later days. This city was built on a hill facing the sea, and was famous for its temple of Astarte. This structure occupied an extensive open court, surrounded by cloisters, and entered from below by staircases. It was crowned by a tall cone-shaped obelisk, the sacred emblem of the goddess. In this shrine the rites of Adonis were also celebrated. In fact the whole city was sacred to him, and the river Nahr Ibrahim, which flows into the sea near Byblus, was known in ancient times as the Adonis River. A dynasty of kings, the Cinyrads, for many generations ruled over Byblus. The last King Cinyras was deposed and sentenced to death by the Roman general, Pompey the Great, for excesses of tyranny. A remote ancestor of this last Cinyras was said to have founded a fane of Astarte atop Mt. Lebanon. The site of this shrine was perhaps at Aphaca, located at the source of the river Adonis, about halfway between Byblus and Baalbek. The sacred grove of Astarte at Aphaca flourished until the fourth century of the Christian era when the Roman emperor Constantine destroyed the sanctuary on account of the orgiastic rites performed

**Saturn (Kronos, Cronos)**

**Astarte**

there. The Vale of Adonis was picturesque, and it was an imposing site for a great pagan sanctuary. Frazer's description of the Vale of Adonis is one of his finest passages:

> The site of the temple has been discovered by modern travelers near the miserable village which still bears the name of Afka at the head of the wild, romantic, wooded gorge of the Adonis. The hamlet stands among groves of noble walnut-trees on the brink of the glen. A little way off the river rushes from a cavern at the foot of a mighty amphitheater of towering cliffs to plunge in a series of cascades into the awful depths of the glen. The deeper it descends, the ranker and denser grows the vegetation, which, sprouting from the crannies and fissures of the rocks, spreads a green veil over the roaring or murmuring stream in the tremendous chasm below. . .The temple, of which some massive hewn blocks and a fine column of Syenite granite still mark the site, occupied a terrace facing the source of the river and commanding a magnificent prospect. Across the foam and the roar of the waterfalls you look up to the cavern and away to the top of the sublime precipices above. So lofty is the cliff that the goats which creep along its ledges to browse on the bushes appear like ants to the spectator hundreds of feet below. Seaward the view is especially impressive when the sun floods the profound gorge with golden light, revealing all the fantastic buttresses and rounded towers of its mountain rampart, and falling softly on the varied green of the woods which clothe its depths. It was here that according to the legend, Adonis met Aphrodite for the first or the last time, and here his mangled body was buried. A fairer scene could hardly be imagined for a story of tragic love and death. Yet, sequestered as the valley is and must always have been, it is not wholly deserted. A convent or a village may be observed here and there standing out against the sky on the top of some beetling crag, or clinging to the face of a nearby perpendicular cliff high above the, foam and the din of the river; and at evening the lights that twinkle through the gloom betray the presence of human habitations on slopes which might seem inaccessible to man. In antiquity the whole of the lovely vale appears to have been dedicated to Adonis, and to

this day it is haunted by his memory; for the heights which shut it in are crested at various points by ruined monuments of his worship, some of them overhanging dreadful abysses, down which it turns the head dizzy to look and see the eagles wheeling about their nests far below. . . Every year, in the belief of his worshippers, Adonis was wounded to death on the mountains, and every year the face of nature itself was dyed with his sacred blood. So year by year the Syrian damsels lamented his untimely fate, while the red anemone, his flower, bloomed among the cedars of Lebanon, and the river ran red to the sea, fringing the winding shores of the blue Mediterranean, whenever the wind set inshore, with a sinuous band of crimson. (Frazer, *Adonis, Attis, Osiris*, Vol. I, pp. 28-30.)

West of Syria, in the Mediterranean Sea, lies the island of Cyprus, only one day's sail from the mainland. On clear summer evenings observers in Syria may have seen the sun setting beyond the mountains of Cyprus. Phoenician invaders settled in Cyprus at an early date and remained there even after the island had succumbed to the sway of the Greeks. The evidences of coins and inscriptions tell us that Phoenician kings reigned at Citium, even down to the time of Alexander the Great. The Phoenician colonists brought north with them their ancient gods. The Baal of the Lebanon was probably Adonis. At Amathus the rites of Adonis and Astarte were established. These ceremonies, like those at Byblus, resembled those of the Osirian cult of Egypt so closely that some people identified the Adonis of Amathus with Osiris. But the great seat of the worship of Adonis and Aphrodite was at Paphos. The temple at Paphos was of considerable antiquity; having been founded, according to Herodotus, by Phoenician colonists from Ascalon. Astarte or Aphrodite was a type of Great Mother goddess, whose sacred symbol was a white cone or pyramid. At certain seasons these sacred stones were anointed with olive oil. This custom still survives among peasants at Paphos who annually anoint the corner stones of the ruined Temple of the Paphian Goddess. These Cypriote peasants, though nominally Christians, still worship the old deities. For instance, in certain chapels these people worship the mother of Christ under the title *Phanaghia Aphroditessa*.

The Easter ceremonies still performed in Greek and Roman Catholic churches in Europe are so similar to ancient rites of the Adonis cult that Sir J. G. Frazer has concluded that these churches actually derived these rites from the ancient worshippers of Adonis.

**Pluto and Persephone (Proserpine)**

**Aphrodite**

**Herodotus (d. 424 B.C.)**

The report by an eyewitness of Good Friday and Easter ceremonies
in an Orthodox Church is given below:

> During the whole of Good Friday a waxen image of the
> dead Christ is exposed to view in the middle of the
> Greek churches and is covered with fervent kisses by
> the thronging crowd, while the whole church rings with
> melancholy, monotonous dirges. Late in the evening,
> when it has grown quite dark, this waxen image is car-
> ried by the priests into the street on a bier adorned with
> lemons, roses, jessamine, and other flowers, and there
> begins a grand procession of the multitude, who move in
> serried ranks, with slow and solemn step, through the
> whole town. Every man carries his taper and breaks out
> into doleful lamentation. At all the houses which the
> procession passes there are seated women with censers
> to fumigate the marching host. Thus the community
> solemnly buries its Christ as if he had just died. At last
> the waxen image is again deposited in the church, and
> the same lugubrious chants echo anew. These lamenta-
> tions, accompanied by a strict fast, continue till mid-
> night, Saturday. As the clock strikes twelve, the bishop
> appears and announces the glad tidings that "Christ is
> risen," to which the crowd replies "He is risen indeed,"
> and at once the whole city bursts into an uproar of joy,
> which finds vent in shrieks and shouts, in endless dis-
> charge of carronades and muskets, and the explosion of
> fireworks of every sort. In the very same hour people
> plunge from the extremity of the fast into the enjoyment
> of the Easter lamb and neat wine. (Sir James George
> Frazer, *The New Golden Bough,* edited by Dr. Theodore
> H. Gaster, New York: Criterion Books, 1959, p. 297.)

Another such first-hand account was recorded by a Sicilian
writer and is descriptive of the Easter ceremonies celebrated in
Roman Catholic churches in Sicily:

> A truly moving ceremony is the procession which
> always takes place in the evening in every commune of
> Sicily, and further the Deposition from the Cross. The
> brotherhoods took part in the procession, and the rear
> was brought up by a great many boys and girls repre-
> senting saints, both male and female, and carrying the
> emblems of Christ's Passion. The Deposition from the

Cross was managed by the priests. The coffin with the dead Christ in it was flanked by Jews armed with swords, an object of horror and aversion in the midst of profound pity excited by the sight not only of Christ but of the Mater Dolorosa, who followed behind him... Sometimes the procession followed the "three hours of agony" and the "Deposition from the Cross." The "three hours" commemorated those which Jesus Christ passed upon the Cross. Beginning at the eighteenth and ending at the twenty-first hour of Italian time two priests preached alternately on the Passion. Anciently the sermons were delivered in the open air on the place called the Calvary; at last when the third hour was about to strike at the words *emisit spiritum,* Christ died, bowing his head among the sobs and tears of the bystanders. Immediately afterwards in some places, three hours afterwards in others, the sacred body was unnailed and deposited in the coffin. In Castronuovo, at the Ave Maria, two priests clad as Jews, representing Joseph of Arimathea and Nicodemus, with their servants in costumes, repaired to the Calvary, preceded by the Company of the Whites. In Salaparuta the Calvary is erected in the Church. At the announcement of the death, the Crucified is made to bow his head by means of machinery while guns are fired, trumpets sound, and amid the silence of the people, impressed by the death of the Redeemer, the strains of a melancholy funeral march are heard. Christ is removed from the Cross and deposited in the coffin by three priests. After the procession of the dead Christ, the burial is performed, that is, two priests lay Christ in a fictitious sepulchre, from which at the mass of Easter Saturday the image of the risen Christ issues and is elevated upon the altar by means of machinery. (Frazer, *The New Golden Bough,* p. 298.)

Commenting on the narrative cited above, Frazer concluded that:

When we reflect how often the Church has skillfully contrived to plant the seeds of the new faith on the old stock of paganism we may surmise that the Easter celebration of the dead and risen Adonis, was, as we have reason to believe, also celebrated in Syria at the same season. The type, created by Greek artists, of the sorrowful goddess with her dying lover in her arms, resembles and may have been the model of the *Pietà*, of Christian art, the Virgin with the dead body of her divine son in her lap, of which the most celebrated example is the one by Michael Angelo in St. Peter's. That noble group, in which the living sorrow of the mother contrasts so wonderfully with languor of death in the son, is one of the finest compositions in marble. Ancient Greek art has bequeathed to us few works so beautiful, and none so pathetic. (Frazer, *Adonis, Attis, Osiris*, Vol. I, pp.256-257.)

Jerome, an early Christian scholar, has transmitted to posterity the fact that at Bethlehem, the traditional birthplace of the Lord, was the seat of a sacred grove dedicated to the worship of Adonis. One of the earliest centers of Orthodox Christianity was at Antioch, and this was another ancient seat of the Adonis Cult.

The Roman emperor Julian visited Antioch while the worshippers of Adonis were celebrating one of their festivals. When the ruler approached the city he was given public prayers and treated as if he were a god. A great multitude cried out that the Star of Salvation had risen in the East. This was undoubtedly the planet Venus, as the Morning Star. Astarte, the divine consort of Adonis, has been identified with the planet Venus. The phases of Venus were carefully noted by Babylonian astronomers, and the annual festival of Adonis was timed to coincide with the appearance of Venus as the Morning or Evening Star. At Antioch the appearance of the Morning Star on the festival day signified the coming of the Goddess of Love to awaken her deceased consort from his state of death. This being the case, we may surmise that it was Venus as the Morning Star which led the wise men of the East to Bethlehem, that sacred spot, which, according to Jerome, witnessed the lament for Adonis and the weeping of the Infant Christ.

In an old Akkadian hymn, the mother of Tammuz is addressed as: "Oh Virgin Ishtar." She was depicted like the Virgin Mary with her divine child in her arms; and, likewise, she was hailed as the Queen of Heaven. Williamson in a scholarly study of religious origins notes that:

According to the Babylonian records, the birth of Tammuz was of miraculous nature. But the most remarkable fact in the whole legend is that he was regarded as both the son and husband of his mother ... though paralleled in the Egyptian and in other religions, this astounding dual relationship is here brought more into view. Can it be that this old Babylonian legend is but an archaic version of the story of the Christian nativity—God the Son incarnating as Jesus Christ, while he is at the same time but another aspect of God the Father? (W. Williamson, *The Great Law — A Study of Religious Origins,* London: Longmans, Green and Co., 1899, pp. 29-30.)

Adonis was a typical Savior-God, and again citing Williamson:

> His death was commemorated annually with mournful chants as his image lay upon a bed or bier. For three days was he bewailed as one dead, but then followed the rejoicing over his resurrection. During the ceremony of the resurrection feast, which took place on the 25th of March, the priest, after having touched the mouths of the mourners with holy oil, murmured: "Trust ye in your Lord, for the pains which he endured have procured your salvation . . . Then the people answered: Hail to the Dove, the restorer of light." (Williamson, *Great Law,* pp. 53-54.)

The myths concerning Attis have much in common with those relating to Adonis. Attis was to Phrygia what Adonis was to Syria. He was a young herdsman or shepherd, beloved by Cybele, the Mother of the Gods, and he was the son of the Virgin Nana. His death was caused either by an encounter with a boar or by self-castration at the foot of a pine tree. The original seat of the Attis Cult was at Pessinus, in Phrygia, but it became prominent in Rome in 204 B.C., when the worship of the Phrygian Great Mother of the Gods was adopted by certain inhabitants of the eternal city. Rome at that time was at war with Carthage; an invading army led by Hannibal was at the gates of Rome. A prophecy of the *Sibylline Books* asserted that the Punic invaders would be driven out of Italy if the goddess Cybele was brought to Rome. Roman ambassadors went to Phrygia and returned with a sacred black stone, emblem of the divinity of the Mother Goddess. This fetish was installed in the Temple of Victory on the Palatine Hill. The citizens of Rome received immediate benefits from this transaction. For as Frazer pointed out:

> It was the middle of April when the goddess arrived, and she went to work at once. For the harvest that year was such as had not been seen for many a

**Attis (Atys)**

long day, and in the very next year Hannibal and his veterans embarked for Africa. As he looked his last on the coast of Italy, fading behind him in the distance, he could not foresee that Europe, which had repelled the arms, would yet, yield to the gods of the Orient. (Frazer, *Adonis, Attis, Osiris*, Vol. I, p. 265.)

In Rome the festival of the death of Attis was celebrated yearly from March 22nd to the 25th, and the influence of this cult on Christianity is undeniable, for in Italy, Gaul and Phrygia, the early Christians adopted March 25th as the date of the passion of Christ.

In the Attis festival a pine tree was felled on the 22nd of March and an effigy of the god was affixed to it, thus being slain and hanged on a tree. The effigy was then entombed. On March 24th, the Day of Blood, the High Priest, impersonating the god, drew blood from his arm, as a substitute for a human sacrifice. At night the priests found the tomb illuminated from within but empty, since on the third day Attis had arisen from the grave. On the 25th of March the resurrection was joyfully celebrated with a sacramental meal, initiates had their sins washed away and were said to be born again. The effects of these rites on Christianity have been well documented. In the words of Weigall:

> There can be no doubt that these ceremonies and beliefs deeply colored the interpretation placed by the first Christians upon the historic facts of the Crucifixion, burial, and coming again to life of Jesus; and indeed, the merging of the worship of Attis into that of Jesus was effected almost without interruption, for these pagan ceremonies were enacted in a sanctuary on the Vatican hill which afterwards was taken over by the Christians, and the mother church of St. Peter now stands upon the very spot. (Sir Arthur Weigall, *The Paganism in Our Christianity*, New York: G. P. Putnam Sons, 1928, p. 123.)

The reader who wishes further information on topics discussed in this chapter is referred to Frazer, *Adonis, Attis, Osiris*.

Mithra

# Chapter VI
# Mithra The Mediator

Mithra, an ancient Iranian sun-god, was born of a virgin on December 25th (Christmas). His first worshippers were shepherds, and he was followed in his travels by twelve companions. The Mithraists observed weekly sabbath days and celebrated the Eucharist by eating wafers marked with a cross. The two great Mithraic festivals were the Birth (Christmas) and the Resurrection (Easter). During the Easter rites, the priests placed an image of Mithra in a tomb. Later the chief priest announced the resurrection of the god by saying: "Be of good cheer, sacred band of Initiates, your god has risen from the dead. His pains and suffering shall be your salvation."

Kersey Graves in *The World's Sixteen Crucified Saviors* says that:

> This god was crucified in Persia in 600 B.C., citing Godfrey Higgins to the effect that he was slain upon the cross to make atonement for mankind, and to take away the sins of the world. This date of 600 B.C. cannot be correct, for Mithra was known among the pre-Aryan Indians at a much earlier date. He may have been a man who was elevated to godhood after his death during the dominance of the Dravidians, who preceded the Aryans of the Vedic age. Mithra was the Mediator between God and Man. He was the great sun-god of the Roman world; but originally he was not a personification of the light of the sun; for it seems that he was a sky-god, originally, and that his identification with the sun came later. Mithraism was the outcome of the blending of Persian dualism and Chaldean stellarism. As to how, when and where Mithra was evolved from a god of light in general into a sun-god in particular we have no certain knowledge. "The change perhaps took place in Babylonia," Frazer surmised, "where, under the powerful influence of Chaldean theology and astrology, the Iranian deities were assimilated to their nearest Semitic counterparts, the supreme god Ahura Mazda being identified

69

with the sky-god Bel, while the goddess Anahita was
confused with Ishtar, the goddess of the planet Venus,
and Mithra was equated with the sun-god Shamash."
(Sir James George Frazer, The *Worship of Nature*,
New York: Macmillan and Co., 1926, p. 503.)

Mithra was one of the minor gods of the Persians, but as the worship spread to Chaldea, Anatolia, and Armenia, he became a major
god. Mithraism became the dominant religion of the ruling classes
of Pontus, Cappadocia, and Syria. In the first century B.C. King
Mithridates Eupator of Pontus, a devout worshipper of Mithra,
engaged in war with the Roman legions. In this struggle
Mithridates was aided by Cilician pirates, whom it seems were converted to Mithraism by their royal patron. Afterwards these pirates
were conquered by the Romans and then converted the Roman soldiers to the worship of the Unconquered Sun. The soldiers carried
this new religion to all parts of the Roman Empire, where it was
adopted by the civilian population and eventually became the dominant religious cult. As to how all this came about, we turn to some
remarks of Frazer, expressed with characteristic charm:

> Outside the Anatolian tableland, the first to
> observe the rites of Mithra, are said to have been the
> Cilician pirates. During the Civil wars which dis
> tracted the attention and absorbed the energies of the
> Romans in the first century of our era, the daring
> rovers seized the opportunity to issue from the secret
> creeks and winding rivers of Cilicia and scour the
> seas, landing from time to time, harrying islands,
> holding cities to ransom, and carrying off from some
> of the most famous sanctuaries the wealth which had
> been accumulated there by the piety of the ages.
> Gorged with plunder and elated by the impunity
> which they long enjoyed, the corsairs rose to an
> extraordinary pitch of audacity and effrontery, march
> ing up the high roads of Italy, plundering villas, and
> abducting Roman magistrates in their robes of office;
> while at sea they displayed pomp and pageantry pro
> portioned to the riches which they had amassed by
> their successful forays. Their galleys flaunted gilded
> sails and purple awnings, and glided along to the
> measured splash of silvered oars, while the sounds of
> music and revelry wafted across the water, told to the
> trembling inhabitants of the neighboring coasts, the

riot and debauchery, of the buccaneers. (Frazer, *The Worship of Nature,* pp. 505-506.)

At the end of the first century B.C. Mithraism was indubitably the dominant cult of the Roman Empire. The poet Statius even suggested that the old sun-god Apollo might be properly addressed as "Mithra, who under the rocks of the Persian cave twists the bull's struggling horns." The poet was here referring to a sculptured scene, carved on many Mithraic monuments widely scattered throughout the Roman Empire. The carving showed Mithra in a cave kneeling on the back of a bull, twisting the head of the same with one hand, and driving a knife into the flank of the animal with the other. In commenting on the sentiments expressed by Statius, the scholiast Lactantius Placidus opined that Mithra was the sun, worshipped in caves in Persia, and that the horned bull was a symbol of the horned moon. This idea was suggestive of an eclipse of the sun caused by the moon coming between the earth and the sun. The same commentator also noted that Mithra was sometimes pictured as lion-headed, a circumstance which he thought related to the entrance of the sun into the zodiacal constellation of Leo the Lion. This last speculation was both ingenious and erroneous, for the lion-headed god was certainly not Mithra. Images of a lion-head deity with a serpent twined around his body and grasping a key or two in his hands was the Persian god Zervan Akarnan (Infinite Time), a personification of Time. A sect of the Magi held that the divinity was the creator of all things and the progenitor of both Ormuzd and Ahriman. Among the numerous monuments showing the bull sacrifice in Mithraic art there are shown two other figures dressed like the god and like him wearing peaked Phrygian caps. These associates of the bull-slaying god were Cautes, holding a burning torch upright, and Cautopates, holding a burning torch downward. We may surmise that Cautes was the rising sun; Mithra, the noon sun; and Cautopates, the setting sun. The dual torchbearers might also be regarded as symbolic of the sun at the vernal and autumnal equinoxes, respectively. On some of the monuments Cautes is shown holding in his hands the head of a bull, or a bull is seen browsing or resting by his side. Cautopates, on the other hand, is displayed with a scorpion either held in his hands or crawling at his feet. Five thousand years ago in ancient Babylonia the sun entered the zodiacal sign of Taurus (The Bull) at the vernal equinox and passed into Scorpio (The Scorpion) at the autumnal equinox. Around three thousand years later in classical Rome in an account of the precession of the equinoxes the sun at the beginning of spring was in Aries (The Ram) and in the sign of Libra (The Balance) at the start of autumn. In the words of Frazer:

It is tempting to conjecture that the traditional emblems of the constellations which once marked the beginning of spring and the beginning of autumn were transmitted from Chaldea to the west and preserved in the symbolism of the mysteries long after they had ceased to correspond with the facts of astronomy. (Frazer, *The Worship of Nature,* p. 516.)

The mysteries of Mithra, like those of many other nations, recruited initiates and educated them through several degrees, or grades. In the Mithraic system there were seven grades, symbolized as:

(1) The Raven,
(2) The Gryphon,
(3) The Soldier,
(4) The Lion,
(5) The Persian,
(6) The Courier of the Sun, and
(7) The Eagle.

Mithraism was dominant in the Roman Empire up until the time when Christianity became the state religion in the fourth century. Many of the beliefs and doctrines of the Mithraists were adopted by the Christians, who conquered their rivals by absorbing them. An example of this is given below by Weigall:

The Hebrew Sabbath having been abolished by the Christians, the Church made a sacred day of Sunday, partly because it was the day of the resurrection but largely because it was the weekly festival of the sun; for it was a definite Christian policy to take over the pagan festivals endeared to the people by tradition, and to give them a Christian significance. But as a solar festival, Sunday was the sacred day of Mithra; and it is interesting to notice that since Mithra was addressed as Dominus (Lord), Sunday must have been the Lord's Day long before Christian times. The head of the Church was the *Papa* or Father, now known as the Pope, who was seated in Rome. The Pope's crown is called a tiara, but a tiara is Persian, and perhaps a Mithraic headdress. The ancient chair preserved in the Vatican and supposed to have been the pontifical throne used by St. Peter is in reality of pagan origin, and may possibly be Mithraic also, for it has upon it certain pagan carvings which are thought to be connected with Mithra. (Weigall, *The Paganism in our Christianity,* pp. 145-146.)

Julian, one of the noblest of the Roman rulers, was a devout sun worshipper. He tried to crush Christianity and restore paganism in the fourth century but failed gloriously. We may regret that he had no success. One of his modern scholarly admirers has paid him this tribute:

> The last stand for the worship of the Sun in antiquity was made by the Roman Emperor Julian. In a rhapsody addressed to the orb of day, the grave and philosophic Emperor professes himself a follower of King Sun. He declares that the Sun is the common Father of all men, since he begat us and feeds us and gives us all good things; there is no single blessing in our lives which we do not receive from him. And Julian concludes his enthusiastic panegyric with a prayer that the Sun, the King of the Universe, would be gracious to him, granting him as a reward, for his pious zeal, a virtuous life and more perfect wisdom, and in due time, an easy and peaceful departure from this life, that he might ascend to his God in Heaven, there to dwell with Him forever. However, the deity to whom he prayed may have granted him a virtuous life, but he withheld from his worshipper the boon of an easy and peaceful end. It was in the press of battle that this last imperial votary of the Sun received his mortal wound, and met a most painful death with the fortitude of a hero and the serenity of a saint. With him, the sun of pagan and imperial Rome set, not ingloriously. (Frazer, *The Worship of Nature,* p. 528.)

**Julian (331-363)**

# Chapter VII
# Prometheus of Greece

One of the prominent themes of Greek mythology was the origin of evil. According to Hesiod (ninth century B.C.), Pandora, wife of Epimenides, owned a box, which the god Zeus had proclaimed should not be opened. Pandora opened her box which was filled with various troubles. These troubles then got loose in the world. Up to this time mankind had been supposed to be immortal. For the inquisitiveness of Pandora, Zeus invoked the curse of death for all humanity. Due to the wickedness of men, Zeus sent a flood to destroy the human race, but there were a few survivors. Prometheus, a creator-god, defied Zeus and became the benefactor of mankind. In order to alleviate the poverty and misery of early humanity, Prometheus stole fire from the sky-world and brought it to earth to serve humanity. This enraged Zeus, who held that fire was a possession of the gods and was not to be given to man, so Prometheus was condemned to be crucified on a crag on the Caucasus mountains. Here he was nailed to an upright beam of timber fitted with extended arms of wood — in other words, a cross. The Greeks regarded Prometheus as a savior of the human race and commemorated his sacrifice by torch races at the Panathenaic games. As Findlay has so well expressed it:

> Instead of being a legendary fire stealer he became to the Greeks their divine Savior and Redeemer, the one who had died to take on his shoulders man's load of guilt, and to suffer in place of humanity ... his worshippers looked upon him as divine and as having come down from heaven to live the life of a god-man. They believed that he was the Creator of the human race, and that on his return to heaven he acted... as the mediator between God and Man... In their art, they represented him as crucified to a rock and wearing a mock crown. (Findlay, *The Psychic Stream*, p. 268.)

The Greek dramatist, Aeschylus (sixth century B.C.), wrote a Passion Play, in which the crucifixion, burial, and resurrection of

**Prometheus**

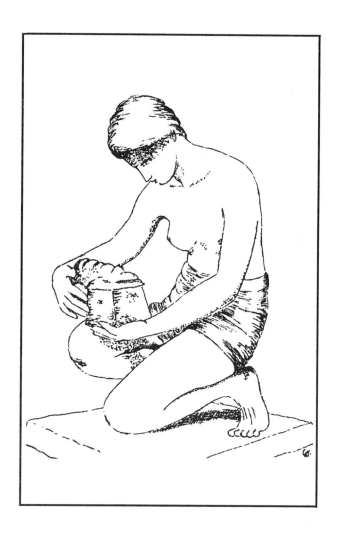

**Pandora**

Prometheus was shown on the stage in Athens. In this dramatic performance an actor, representing Prometheus, hung on a cross in the theater, made the following speech:

Who ever thou art, a hapless god thou seest, nailed to this crag, the foe of Zeus thou seest. Him thou seest, whom all the immortals who so tread the Olympian threshold, name with hatred. Yet thou beholdest man's best friend, and hated for excessive love.

Soon as Zeus sat on his ancestral throne, he called the gods together, and assigned to each his fair allotment and his sphere of sway supreme, but all for wretched man to him no part or portion fall. Zeus vowed to blot his memory from earth, and mold the race anew.

I, Prometheus, only of the gods, did thwart his will and but for my strong aid Hades had overwhelmed and hopeless ruin swamped all men that breathe, such were my crimes. These pains, grievous to suffer, pitiful to behold, were purchased thus, and mercy's now denied to him whose crime was mercy to mankind.

And here I hang, in cunning torment stretched, a spectacle inglorious to Zeus.

The scene enacted in Athens 500 years B.C. recalls to mind the Biblical story of how Jesus Christ on the cross called out in agony: "My God, my God, why hast thou forsaken me?"

# Chapter VIII
# Krishna and Buddha of India

Krishna was the eighth Avatar of the Hindu pantheon and is said to have lived about 1200 B.C. The parallels between the life of Krishna, as recorded in the sacred books of India, and of the life of Jesus Christ, as related in the sacred anthology of the Christians, is so close that some scholars have believed that the Christian writers copied their account from the Hindus. This opinion, though plausible, has little to recommend it; the most we can say is that both traditions seem to be traceable to a common source. In this brief sketch only a few of these parallels can be discussed. (For an exhaustive treatment the reader is referred to John M. Robertson, *Christianity and* Mythology, London: Watts and Company, 1936.)

The Hindu Christ, like many other savior-gods, was born of a virgin. Krishna was the son of the Virgin Devaki. An angelic voice from heaven announced to the Virgin: "In thy delivery, O favored among women, all nations shall have cause to rejoice." The nativity of Krishna was heralded by a star at the time of his birth in a cave, where he was visited by wise men who brought him valuable presents. In the Apocryphal Gospel "Protevangelion," a work attributed to James the brother of Jesus, we have been told that the Christian Savior was also born in a cave. At the time of the birth of Krishna the cave was mysteriously illuminated. Similarly, at the birth of Jesus there was such a bright light in the cave that the eyes of Joseph and the midwife could not bear it. (This tradition has been recorded in *The Apocryphal New Testament: Gospel of Protevangelion,* Chapter 14:11.) The infant Krishna began speaking to his mother soon after his birth. In *The New Testament Apocrypha* we read a similar story about Jesus. In this document we have been told that:

> Jesus spake even when he was in the cradle, and said to his mother: "Mary, I am Jesus, the Son of God, that WORD which thou didst bring forth according to the declaration of the angel Gabriel to thee, and my Father hath sent me for the salvation of the world."
> *(The First Gospel of the Infancy,* Chapter 1:2, 3.)

The birth of Krishna occurred while his foster father, Nanda, was in the city to pay his tax to the King. Likewise, Jesus was born while his foster father, Joseph, was in the city to pay tax to the governor.

King Kansa sought the life of the Hindu Christ by ordering the slaughter of all male children born on the same night as was Krishna. This is paralleled by the story of the slaughter of the innocents, ordered by King Herod, as related in the Gospel according to Matthew: 2-16.

A heavenly voice warned Nanda to flee across the Jumna River with the infant Krishna in order to escape from King Kansa. In this instance, we recall that Joseph was warned in a dream to flee into Egypt with the Virgin Mary and the Christ-child to escape from King Herod.

Krishna performed numerous miracles in Mathura. While in Egypt, Jesus performed similar miracles in Matarea.

Krishna was the second person of the Hindu Trinity, which consisted of (1) Brahma, (2) Vishnu, and (3) Siva. Krishna was the human incarnation of Vishnu. As we know, Jesus Christ was recognized as the second person of the Christian Trinity.

Krishna, according to tradition, was a crucified Christ. He is pictured in Indian art as hanging on a cross with arms extended. In the words of Dr. Thomas Inman: "Krishna, whose history so closely resembles our Lord's, was also like him in his being crucified." (Thomas Inman, M.D., *Ancient Faiths*, Vol. I, p. 411, cited by Doane in *Bible Myths and Their Parallels in Other Religions*, p. 186.)

At the crucifixion Krishna was wounded by an arrow. Similarly, Jesus was pierced by a spear.

The light of the sun was blotted out at noontime on the day of Krishna's death. The correlative Bible account records the darkening of the sun from the sixth to the ninth hour on the day of the crucifixion of the Christian Christ. This darkness at the Passion of Jesus Christ was commented upon by the historian, Edward Gibbon, in the following words:

> But how shall we excuse the supine inattention of the Pagan and philosophic world, to those evidences which were presented by the hand of Omnipotence, not to their reason, but to their senses? During the age of Christ, of his apostles, and of their first disciples, the doctrine which they had preached was confirmed by innumerable prodigies. The lame walked, the blind saw, the sick were healed, the dead were raised, demons were expelled, and the laws of Nature

**Krishna**

**Brahma**

**Vishnu**

**Siva**

were frequently suspended for the benefit of the Church. But the sages of Greece and Rome turned aside from the awful spectacle, and, pursuing the ordinary occupations of life and study, appeared unconscious of any alteration in the moral or physical government of the world. Under the reign of Tiberius, the whole earth, or at least a celebrated province of the Roman Empire, was involved in a preternatural darkness of three hours. Even this miraculous event, which ought to have excited the wonder, the curiosity, and the devotion of mankind, passed without notice in an age of science and history. It happened during the lifetime of Seneca and the elder Pliny, who must have experienced the immediate effects, or received the earliest intelligence, of the prodigy. Each of these philosophers, in a laborious work, has recorded all of the great phenomena of nature, earthquakes, meteors, comets, and eclipses, which his indefatigable curiosity could collect. Both the one and the other have omitted to mention the greatest phenomenon to which the mortal eye has been witness since the creation of the globe. A distinct chapter of Pliny is designed for eclipses of an extraordinary nature and duration; but he contents himself with describing the singular defect of light which followed the murder of Caesar, when, during the greatest part of a year, the orb of the sun appeared pale and without splendor. This season of obscurity, which cannot surely be compared with the preternatural darkness of the Passion, had been already celebrated by most of the poets and historians of the memorable age. (Edward Gibbon, *History of Christianity,* New York: Peter Eckler Publishing Co., 1923, pp. 200-202.)

The descent into hell was one of the exploits of Krishna, where he raised the dead before returning to the abode of the gods. On the return from hell, he brought with him two boys whom he restored to their Parents on earth. In *The New Testament Apocrypha* is an account of the descent of the Christian Savior into hell, from whence he led a party of saints back to earth, and besides them, two sons of the high priest, who were returned to life on earth. The story of the descent into hell is related in the *Gospel of Nicodemus*, from which the following extracts are taken:

Satan, the prince and captain of death, said to the Prince of Hell, "Prepare to receive Jesus of Nazareth, himself who boasted that he was the Son of God, and yet was a man afraid of death." . . . To this the Prince of hell replied to Satan; "Who is that so powerful prince, and yet a man who is afraid of death?" . . . And while Satan and the Prince of Hell were discoursing thus to each other, on a sudden there was a voice as of thunder and the rushing of winds, saying, "Lift up your gates, O ye princes; and be ye lift up, O everlasting gates, and the King of Glory shall come in." When the Prince of Hell heard this, he said to Satan, "Depart from me and begone out of my habitations; if thou art a powerful warrior, fight with the King of Glory. But what hast thou to do with him?" And then he cast him forth from his habitations. And the prince said to his impious officers, "Shut the brass gates of cruelty and make them fast with iron bars, and fight courageously, lest we be taken captives." But when all the company of the saints heard this they spake with a loud voice of anger to the Prince of Hell, "Open thy gates that the King of Glory may come in." . . . Then there was a great voice, as of the sound of thunder, saying, "Lift up your gates, O princes; and be ye lifted up, ye gates of hell, and the King of Glory will enter in." The Prince of Hell, perceiving the same voice repeated, cried out...Who is that King of Glory?" David replied to the Prince of Hell,..."I say unto thee, the Lord strong and powerful, the Lord mighty in battle; he is the King of Glory, and he is the Lord in heaven and earth. He hath looked down to hear the groans of the prisoners, and to set loose those that are appointed to death. And now, thou filthy and stinking Prince of Hell, open thy gates, that the King of Glory may enter in; for he is the Lord of heaven and earth." While David was saying this, the mighty Lord appeared in the Form of a man, and enlightened those places which had ever before been in darkness, and broke asunder the fetters which before could not be broken; and with his invincible power visited those who sate in the deep darkness by iniquity, and the shadow of death by sin . . . Then the Prince of Hell took Satan, and with great indignation said to him, "O thou prince of destruction, author of Beelzebub's defeat and banishment, the scorn of God's angels and loathed by all righteous persons! What inclined thee to act thus?" . . While the Prince of Hell was thusly speaking to Satan, the King of Glory said to Beelzebub, the Prince of Hell, "Satan the prince shall be subject to thy dominion forever, in the room of Adam and his righteous sons, who are mine." Then Jesus stretched forth his hand, and said, "Come to me, all ye saints, who are created in my image, who were condemned by the tree of the forbidden fruit, and by the devil and death; live now by the wood of my cross; the devil, the prince of this world, is overcome and death is conquered." (Dr. Paul Carus, "The Gospel of Nicodemus," *The History of The Devil,* Chicago: Open Court Publishing Co., 1900, pp. 174-179.)

Gautama Buddha, the ninth Avatar of India, flourished around 600 B.C. The stories relating to his life and death are similar to those recorded concerning Krishna. He was said to have been born of the Virgin Maya, or Mary. His incarnation was accomplished by the descent of the Holy Ghost upon the Virgin Maya. The infant Buddha, soon after birth, spoke to his mother, saying: "I will put to an end the sufferings and sorrows of the world." As these words were uttered a mystical light surrounded the infant Messiah. During his earthly pilgrimage the Buddha was tempted by Mara, the evil One, but he heeded not the devil, saying, "Be gone; hinder me not." In the words of Graves:

He believed and taught his followers that all sin is inevitably punished, either in this or the future life; and so great were his sympathy and tenderness, that he condescended to suffer that punishment himself, by an ignominious death upon the cross after which he descended into Hades (Hell), to suffer for a time (three days) for the inmates of that dreadful and horrible prison, that he might show he sympathized with them. After his ascension to heaven, as well as during his earthly sojourn, he imparted to the world some beautiful, lofty, and soul-elevating precepts. (Graves, *The World's Sixteen Crucified Saviors,* p. 116.)

Anyone interested in the life of Buddha should consult Sir Edwin Arnold's *The Light of Asia* (London and New York:George Routledge and Sons, 1879), a biography of Gautama Buddha written as poetry.

**Buddha**

To give an example, when Buddha went out into the world to teach his doctrine, he found himself confronted with much evil.

About the painted temple peacocks flew, the blue doves cooed from every well, far off the village drums beat for some marriage-feast; all things spoke peace and plenty and the Prince saw and rejoiced. But, looking deep, he saw the thorns which grow upon this rose of life: How the swart peasant sweated for his wage, toiling for leave to live; and how he urged the great-eyed oxen through the flaming hours, goading their velvet flanks: then marked he, too, how lizard fed on ant, and snake on him, and kite on both; and how the fish-hawk robbed the fish-tiger of that which it had seized; the shrike chasing the bulbul, which did chase the jeweled butterflies; till everywhere each slew a slayer and in turn was slain, life living upon death. So the fair show veiled one vast, savage, grim conspiracy of mutual murder, from the worm of man, who himself kills his fellow. (Arnold, *The Light of Asia*, pp. 28-29.)

Gautama the Buddha met a mother who was grieving the death of her infant son. The sorrowing mother requested the Master to bring her child back to life, and he answered: "They who seek physicians bring to them what is ordained. Therefore, I pray thee, find black mustard seed, a tola; only mark thou take it not from any hand or house where father, mother, child, or slave hath died; it shall be well if thou canst find such seed."

The mother went away, then later returned and addressed Buddha:

I went, Lord, clasping to my breast the babe, grown colder, asking at each hut — here in the jungle, and towards the town — I pray you, give me mustard of your grace, a tola — black; and each who had it gave, for all the poor are piteous to the poor; but when I asked, "In my friend's household here hath any peradventure ever died — husband, or wife, or child, or slave?" They said: "O Sister! What is this you ask? The dead are very many, and the living few!" So with sad thanks I gave the mustard back, and prayed of others; but the others said, "Here is the seed, but we have lost our slave!" "Here is the seed, but our good man is dead!" "Here is some seed, but he that sowed it died between the rain-time and the harvesting!" Ah, sir! I could not find a single house where there was mustard seed and none had died! . . .

"My sister! Thou hast found," the master said, "Searching for what none find — that bitter balm I had to give thee. He thou lovedst slept dead on thy bosom yesterday: today thou know'st the whole wide world weeps with thy woe: the grief which all hearts share grows less for one. Lo! I would pour my blood if it could stay thy tears and win the secret of that curse which makes sweet love our anguish, and which drives o'er flowers and pastures to the sacrifice — as these dumb beasts are driven — men their lords. I seek that secret: bury thou thy child!" (Arnold, *The Light of Asia,* pp. 127-129.)

(On the extensive parallels between the careers of Gautama Buddha and Jesus Christ the reader might consult, with profit, Doane, Chapter 29 of *Bible Myths.*)

# Chapter IX
# Osiris and Horus of Egypt

The Osiris-Horus cult can be traced back to the Ethiopian ancestors of the Egyptians. In the words of Cooke:

> The worship and rites of Osiris may have passed into Egypt, I think, from the neighboring state of Ethiopia . . . Herodotus says in his history, that following the Nile to the south, you will come to a great city, Meroë. The people there have but two gods — that is, Zeus and Dionysus or Bacchus . . . Now Zeus must be Amen or Amun. Dionysus is no doubt Osiris. . . . The singular paucity of gods may well argue an older tradition than any of which Egypt could boast. (Harold P. Cooke, *Osiris: A Study of Myths, Mysteries and Religion,* London: The C. W. Daniel Co., 1931, p. 154.)

Despite the passage of time, the ancient gods are still worshipped in Egypt.

> That the influence of the ancient faith is not yet dead is shown by Egyptian women in the Delta who are in labor calling on Amoon (Amon) for help, a practice which occurred as late as 1945, giving this religion an effective life of well over six thousand years. Had it not been for its tragic disintegration between 600 B.C. and 450 B.C. under the Greek influence, we should doubtless have had access to many more records of Egypt's past." (Egerton Sykes, *Every-man's Dictionary of Non-Classical Mythology,* 3rd ed., London: J. M. Dent and sons, 1968, p. *xi.*)

On the Ethiopian origin of Osirianism, we have a positive assertion by Diodorus:

> Now the Ethiopians, as historians relate, were the first of all men, and the proofs of this statement, they say, are manifest. For that they did not come into

**Osiris**

**Dionysus (Bacchus)**

**Bacchus and Venus**

**Amen (Amen-ra or Ammon)**

their land as immigrants from abroad, but were the natives of it, and so justly bear the name of autochthones (sprung from the soil itself), is, they maintain, conceded by practically all men....They say also that the Egyptians are colonists sent out by the Ethiopians, Osiris having been the leader of the colony. For, speaking generally, what is now Egypt, they maintain, was not land but sea, when in the beginning the universe was being formed. Afterwards, however, as the Nile during the time of its inundation carried down the mud from Ethiopia, land was gradually built up from the deposit ...and the larger part of the customs of the Egyptians are, they hold, Ethiopian, the colonists still preserving their ancient manners. (Diodorus Siculus *Library of History*, Vol. II, Book III, trans. by C. H. Oldfather, Loeb Classical Library, Boston, Mass.: Harvard University Press, 1933-35, pp. 89-95.)

The mythology and symbolism relative to Osiris and Horus is rather complicated, but we shall try to understand it. In ancient Egypt the kings were gods; the living king was the Horus and the dead king was the Osiris. In the words of Professor G. B. Foucart, French Egyptologist:

The king of Egypt has never been merely a representative or interpreter of the supreme god, or his vicar. Either he is the god himself, manifest on earth in a human body...or he is the god's own son. (Hastings' *Encyclopedia of Religion and Ethics*, Vol. VII, p. 712.)

A clearer explanation of these facts was given by Professor Hocart:

The myth of Osiris is the record of the killing of a king, and is extremely early. Osiris, after his death, became a king in the Underworld...Osiris is killed and becomes King of the Underworld, and from his dead body his successor, Horus, is conceived. But every dead king is Osiris and every living king Horus. Thus Osiris and Horus are really the same, Horus being the living form of Osiris, and Osiris the dead form of Horus. There is thus a succession of men who are killed, become gods, and are succeeded by their posthumous sons. When the

**Horus**

king is allowed to die a natural death, or is not killed
till his powers fail, a pretense will still be made of killing him at what was the proper time, and his son will
therefore be born not from a really dead man, but from
a fictitiously dead man. Hence the ceremonies which
effect the rebirth of the king will be carried out in the
king's own lifetime; he participates as a living man in
the birth ceremonies. Or on the other hand, his successor may have to await his death before he can be reborn
and then, as happens in some African tribes, he will be
reborn not as a babe but as an adult. (A. M. Hocart,
*Social Origins,* London: Watts and Co., 1954, pp. 79-82.)

Osiris was a son of the sky-goddess Nut, who was the wife of the
sun-god Ra. But Ra was not the father of Osiris. The father of Osiris
was the earth-god Seb. On discovery of the infidelity of his wife, Ra
placed a curse on her, predicting that her expected child would be
born in no month and no year. Meanwhile Nut had acquired a new
lover, the god Thoth. This deity had played a game of draughts with
the moon and had won from the orb of night one seventy-second
part of each day of the year; and these fractional parts were com-
pounded into five whole days and were added by Thoth to the
Egyptian year of 360 days. This was a mythological way of account-
ing for the five supplementary days which were added to the
Egyptian year in order to bring the lunar and solar calendars into
agreement. Since the five extra days were regarded as outside of
the year of twelve months, the curse of Ra did not apply to them.
Osiris was born on the first of the supplementary days, and at his
nativity a mysterious voice was heard announcing the earthly
advent of the LORD OF ALL. Osiris was not an only child; on the
second supplementary day Nut gave birth to the elder Horus; she
became the mother of Set on the third day, the goddess Isis on the
fourth day, and the goddess Nephthys on the fifth day. After a while,
Set married his sister Nephthys, and Osiris married his sister Isis.

Then Osiris forsook the realm of the gods and became a king on
earth. He found the inhabitants of Egypt in the savage state and
conferred on them the blessings of civilization. The dwellers by the
Nile had been cannibals before the advent of Osiris. Queen Isis
found wheat and barley growing wild on the banks of the great
river, and King Osiris then introduced the cultivation of these grains
to the people, who then abandoned cannibalism and accommodated
themselves to a diet of corn. Osiris was the first gatherer from
trees; he trained creeping vines to wrap themselves around poles
and was the first to tread the grapes to make wine. The great king

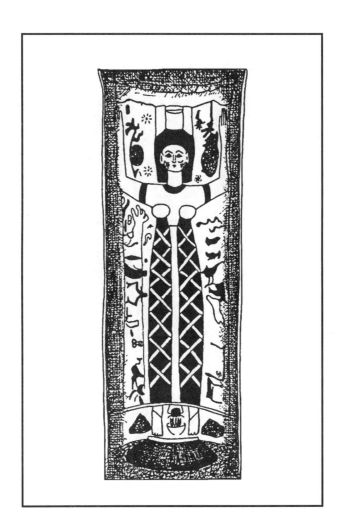

**Nut**

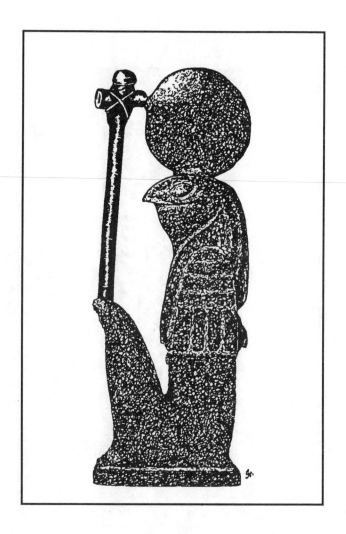

**Ra**

**Seb**

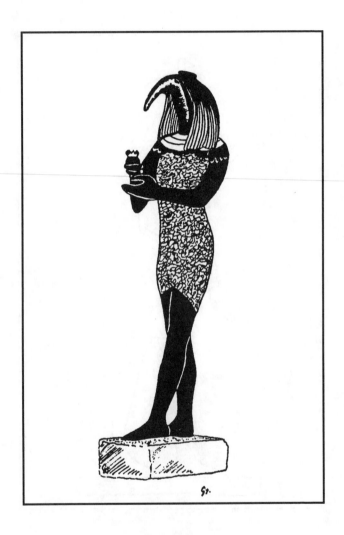

**Thoth**

**Set**

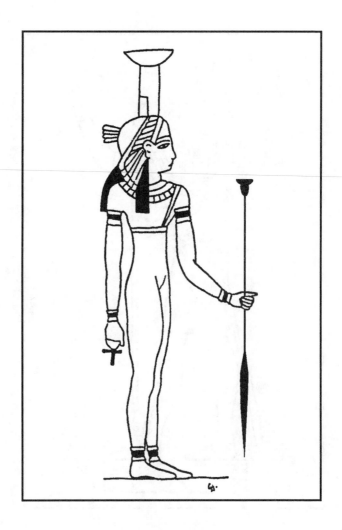

**Nephthys**

**Isis**

then turned over the government of Egypt to his queenly wife, Isis, while he traveled around the world distributing the blessings of agriculture to all mankind. In lands where soil and climate were not suited to the cultivation of the vine, the people were taught to brew beer from barley.

After returning to Egypt, the benevolent monarch, due to the blessings he had conferred on humanity, was hailed as a god and was thus worshipped by a grateful populace. But, sad to say, Osiris had an evil and jealous brother, Set, who along with seventy-two accomplices, plotted the death of Osiris. By guile Set obtained the measurements of his brother's body and constructed a coffer or chest of the same dimensions. Later, at a banquet, Set displayed the coffer and offered to give it to anyone whose body would exactly fit into it. Among all those present none fitted into the chest but Osiris. Then the conspirator closed the lid of the coffer, fastened it with nails, sealed it with molten lead, and set it adrift on the waters of the Nile. All this happened on the 17th day of the month Athyr, when the sun entered the zodiacal sign of Scorpio, and in the 28th year of the reign of Osiris.

The sorrowing widow, Isis, thereafter exiled herself in the papyrus swamps of the Delta where she gave birth to a son, the younger Horus. In the meantime the floating coffin of Osiris had drifted into the Mediterranean Sea and finally landed on the coast of Phoenicia. At this place a mysterious tree appeared and enclosed the coffer in its trunk. The local ruler so admired this tree that he ordered it cut down and fashioned into a pillar for his palace at Byblus. Isis, searching for the body of her deceased husband, in due time arrived at Byblus. The tree-pillar was split by Isis, who recovered the body of Osiris. The pillar was wrapped in fine linen by Isis, who poured ointment over it, and presented it to the King of Byblus. The sacred pillar was set up in a temple of Isis where it was worshipped by the people of Byblus.

The body of Osiris was taken back to Egypt by Isis and there hidden in a secret place. But one evening while Set was hunting boars by the light of the full moon, he chanced to discover the hidden chest, and after opening the same, he seized the body of Osiris, chopped it into fourteen pieces, and scattered them all over the land of Egypt. Isis later made a search and found all the parts of Osiris except one. Each fragment was buried where found, which explains why so many cities in Egypt claimed the grave of Osiris. The missing part, the phallus, was made into an image by Isis for use in the religious myth of Osiris, as related by Plutarch in his treatise, *On Isis and Osiris,* along with some fragments from literature of Ancient Egypt.

**Plutarch (48-122 A.D.)**

**Anubis**

The Osirian story has a happier ending in some of the native Egyptian versions which supplement the narrative of Plutarch. One story tells that after Isis had collected the fragments of the corpse of Osiris, she and her sister Nephthys sat down and cried. This lament was heard by the sun-god Ra, who out of sympathy sent down from heaven the jackal-headed god, Anubis, who with the help of Horus, Isis, Nephthys, and ibis-headed Thoth, reassembled the body of Osiris from the fragments and made the corpse into a mummy. Isis then sprouted wings and fanned the mummy with them. The breath of life returned to Osiris, who arose from death, and then retired to the underworld to reign as King of the Dead. His son Horus, having reached his maturity, became a king and ruled on earth.

The resurrection of Osiris is shown in a series of bas-reliefs on the walls of his temple at Denderah. We see the dead king as a mummy on his bier; he arises gradually, and then he stands erect between the guardian wings of Isis, who stands behind him. In front of the risen god we see a male figure holding up a *crux ansata*, the symbol of eternal life. Another representation of this mystery is depicted in the Temple of Isis at Philae. Here there is an inscription, reading: "This the form of him whom one may not name, Osiris of the Mysteries, who springs from the returning waters." Gods and heroes born of virgins were quite common in days of old, and the source of most, if not all of the virgin-born, dying and resurrecting gods seems to have been Egypt. An English scholar, Jocelyn Rhys, has an interesting statement relating thereto:

> Horus was said to be the parthenogenetic child of the Virgin Mother Isis. In the catacombs of Rome, black statues of this Egyptian divine Mother and Infant still survive from the early Christian worship of the Virgin and Child to which they were converted. In these the Virgin Mary is represented as a black Negress and often, with the face veiled in the true Isis fashion . . . Statues of the goddess Isis with the child Horus in her arms were common in Egypt, and were exported to all neighboring and to many remote countries, where they are still to be found with new names attached to them — Christian in Europe, Buddhist in Turkestan, Taoist in China and Japan. Figures of the Virgin Isis do duty as representations of Mary, of Hariti, of Kuan-Yin, of Kwannon and of other Virgin Mothers of Gods. (Jocelyn Rhys, *Shaken Creeds: The Virgin Birth Doctrine,* London: Watts and Company, 1922, pp. 115-116.)

To some readers these opinions may seem farfetched, but I have no doubt of their validity. A similar view has been expressed by a more recent authority:

> In Roman times the worship of Isis was widespread on all the main lines of communication in Europe, usually in ports and important market towns on rivers. With the advent of Christianity many of the chapels of Isis were taken over, and the representations of the goddess with the infant Horus in her arms became pictures of the Virgin Mary carrying the Holy Child. As Isis was dark-skinned, they became famous Black Virgins. Notre Dame in Paris was built on the remains of a Temple of Isis; the original name of the city was *Para Isidos*, the Grove of Isis. There are Black Virgins near Marseilles, near Barcelona, at Czestochowa in Poland, and in numerous other cities in Europe. (Egerton Sykes, *Everyman's Dictionary of Non-Classical Mythology,* p. 249.)

On the inner walls of the holy of holies in the Temple of Luxor inscribed by King Amenhotep 111(1538–1501 B.C.) the birth of Horus is pictured in four scenes very much like Christian representations of the Annunciation and the Immaculate Conception of the Virgin Mary, and the Birth and Adoration of the Christ Child. These four consecutive scenes, as engraved on the walls of the Temple of Luxor, are reproduced in Gerald Massey's *Ancient Egypt: The Light of the World,* Vol.II (London: T. Fisher Unwin, 1907), p. 757, and may be described as follows:

### The Annunciation
The god Thoth is shown announcing to the Virgin Isis the impending birth of her son, Horus.

### The Immaculate Conception
The god Kneph (the Holy Ghost) and the goddess Hathor are shown mystically impregnating the virgin by holding crosses (symbols of life) to the head and nostrils of the mother-to-be.

### The Birth of The Child God
The mother sits on the midwife's stool, and the newborn infant is held by attendants.

Luxor Temple

### The Adoration

The infant Horus is shown receiving homage from
gods and men, including the Three Kings, or Magi,
who are tendering him gifts. In this scene the cross
symbol again appears. "In this picture," as one
Egyptologist noted, "we have the Annunciation, the
Conception, the Birth and the Adoration as described
in the first and second chapters of Luke's Gospel, and
as we have historical assurance that the chapters in
Matthew's Gospel which contain the miraculous birth
of Christ are after additions not the earliest manu-
scripts, it seems probable that these two poetical
chapters in Luke may also be unhistorical, and borrowed from the Egyptian accounts of the miraculous
birth of their kings." (Samuel Sharpe, *Egyptian
Mythology and Egyptian Christianity*, London: J. R.
Smith, 1879, p. 19.)

The ancient Egyptians worshipped several gods named Horus.
Over a period of thousands of years the various Horuses blended
together until there were only two left: Horus the Sun-god and
Horus the son of Osiris and Isis. The principal Horus gods were as
follows:

### Horus the Elder

This god was worshipped chiefly in a temple at
Ombos in Upper Egypt. His image was that of a man
with the head of a hawk, as a hawk, or as a lion.

### Horus the Younger

He was represented as a youth with a lock of hair
on the right side of the head. (This was called the
Horus lock and symbolized youth.) This Horus wore
the double crown of the two Egypts.

### Horus of the Two Eyes

His images showed a man with a hawk's head upon
which were the horns of a ram, the solar disk, and a
coiled serpent (the *Uraeus*). In each hand of this
Horus was an Utchat, symbols of the all seeing eyes of
the Sun-god.

### The Blind Horus
Known as Horus, Lord of Not Seeing, which symbolized the Sun in eclipse.

### Horus of the Two Horizons
This was the rising and setting sun, symbolized by the Sphinx.

### The Golden Horus
God of the morning sun, or the dawn.

### Horus of Edfu
This Horus was the Sun of the southern heavens at Midday, exemplifying the greatest power and heat of the sun.

### Horus, Son of Isis, Son of Osiris
"In Egyptian mythology it is necessary to distinguish Horus, the sun-god, from Horus, the son of Isis and Osiris. Originally these two deities, both named Horus, appear to have had nothing in common, but in later times an attempt was made to blend them into one . . . Generally speaking, the sun-god Horus can be distinguished from his namesake, the son of Osiris, by the possession of certain titles, which varied with the provinces or cities in which he was worshipped. In the course of time each of the different forms of the sun-god Horus, discriminated from the rest by a distinct epithet, came to be regarded as an independent divinity, and we often find several such duplicate deities worshipped contemporaneously, as if they had no relation to each other, in the later periods of Egyptian history." (Frazer, *The Worship of Nature*, p. 566-567.)

The Horus gods are discussed at length in Sir E. A. Wallis Budge, *The Gods of the Egyptians,* Vol. I (London: Methuen and Co., 1905), pp. 566-599.

The close parallels of the careers of Horus and Jesus Christ are listed in the appendix to Gerald Massey's *Ancient Egypt.* This compendium gives nearly 200 similarities and identities. Dr. Albert Churchward, one of Massey's disciples, has extracted a few of these parallels, which are listed below:

## Horus and Jesus

Horus had two mothers: Isis the Virgin, who conceived him, and Nephthys, who nursed him. He was brought forth singly as one of five brothers.

Jesus had two mothers, Mary the Virgin, who conceived him and Mary, the wife of Cleophas, who brought him forth as one of her children. He was brought forth singly as one of five brethren.

Horus was the son of Seb, his father on earth.

Jesus was the son of Joseph, his father on earth.

Horus was with his mother, the Virgin, until twelve years old, when he was transformed into the beloved son of God as the only begotten of the Father in Heaven.

Jesus remained with his mother, the Virgin, up to the age of twelve years, when he left her "to be about his Father's business."

From twelve to thirty years of age there is no record in the life of Horus.

From twelve to thirty years of age there is no record in the life of Jesus.

Horus, at thirty years of age, became adult in his baptism by Anup.

Jesus, at thirty years of age, was made a man in his baptism by John the Baptist.

Horus in his baptism made his transformation into the beloved son and only begotten of the Father, the Holy Spirit, represented by a bird.

Jesus in his baptism is hailed from Heaven as the beloved son and the only begotten of the Father, God, the Holy Spirit, that is represented by a dove.

The data listed above are from Albert Churchward, *The Signs and Symbols of Primordial Man*, pp. 422-423. For correlative information the reader should consult Gerald Massey's *Lectures* (New York: Weiser, 1974), pp. 1-25.

Concerning the eighteen-year gap in the lives of Horus and Jesus, where there is no record between the ages of twelve and thirty, Massey gave a scholarly explanation, which follows:

### Jesus and Horus
### at Twelve and Thirty Years of Age

The first Horus was the child, who always remained a child. In Egypt the boy or girl wore the Horus-lock of childhood until twelve years of age. Thus childhood ended about the twelfth year. But although adultship was then entered upon . . . the full adultship was not attained until thirty years of age . . . as with the man so it is with the god, and the second Horus, the same god in his second character, is the *Khemt* or *Khem-Horus,* the typical adult of thirty years. The god up to twelve years was Horus the son of Isis, the mother's child. The virile Horus, the adult of thirty years, was representative of the Fatherhood, and this Horus is the anointed son of Osiris. These two characters of Horus the child and Horus the adult of thirty years are reproduced in the two phases to which the life of Jesus is limited in the gospels . . . Thus from the time.when the child-Christ was about twelve years of age until that of the typical *hommefait* of Egypt, which was the age assigned to Horus when he became the adult god, there is no history. This is in exact accordance with the Kamite allegory of the double Horus. And the mythos alone will account for the chasm which is wide and deep enough to engulf a supposed history of eighteen years. Childhood cannot be carried beyond the twelfth year, and the child-Horus always remained a child, just as the child-Christ does in Italy and in the German folk-tales. The mythical record, founded on nature, went no further, and there the history consequently halts within the prescribed limits, to rebegin with the anointed and regenerated Christ at the age of Khem-Horus, the adult of thirty years. (Gerald Massey, *The Historical Jesus and The Mythical Christ,* Star Publishing Co., Springfield, Mass., 1886, pp. 56–58.)

The Egyptian influence on Orthodox Christianity is far more profound than most people realize. All of us have seen the CHI(X)-RHO(P) emblem displayed in many Christian churches, and reputed to be the sacred monogram of Christ. This monogram, originally sacred to Horus, was known in Egypt thousands of years before the beginning of Christianity. The whole Christian Bible was derived from the sacred books of Egypt, such as: *The Book of the Dead, The Pyramid Texts,* and *The Books of Thoth.* In the words of a distinguished American disciple of Gerald Massey, Dr. Alvin Boyd Kuhn:

The entire Christian Bible, creation legend, descent into and exodus from Egypt, ark and flood allegory, Israelite history, Hebrew prophecy and poetry, Gospels, Epistles and Revelation imagery, all are now proven to have been the transmission of ancient Egypt's scrolls and papyri into the hands of later generations which knew neither their true origin nor their fathomless meaning. Long after Egypt's voice, expressed through the inscribed hieroglyphics, was hushed in silence, the perpetuated relics of Hamitic wisdom, with their cryptic message utterly lost, were brought forth and presented to the world by parties of ignorant zealots as a new body of truth . . . from the scrolls of papyri five thousand to ten thousand years old there comes stalking forth to view the whole story of an Egyptian Jesus raising from the dead an Egyptian Lazarus at an Egyptian Bethany, with two Egyptian Manes present, the non-historical prototype of the incident related (only) in John's Gospel. From the walls of the temple of Luxor...there faces Christianity a group of four scenes that spell the non-historicity of four episodes purveyed as history in the Gospel's recital of the Christ's nativity: the angel's pronouncement to the shepherds tending their flocks by night in the fields; the annunciation of the angel to the virgin; the adoration of the infant by three Magi; and the nativity scene itself. Egypt had used the symbol of a star rising in the east as the portent of coming deity for millennia anterior to the Christian era. Egypt had knelt at the shrine of the Madonna and Child, Isis and Horus, for long centuries before a historical Mary lifted a historical Jesus in her arms. Egypt had from remote times adored a Christ who had raised the dead and healed the lame, halt, blind, paralytic, leprous and all afflicted, who had restored speech to the dumb, exorcised demons from the possessed, dispersed his enemies with a word or look, wrestled with his Satan adversary, overcame all temptation and performed the works of his heavenly Father to the victorious end. Egypt had long known a Jesus, Iusa, who had been born amid celestial portents of an immaculate parenthood, circumcised, baptized, tempted, glorified on the mount, persecuted,

**Satan**

arrested, tried, condemned, crucified, buried, resurrected and elevated to heaven. Egypt had listened to the Sermon on the Mount and the sayings of Iusa for ages. Egypt had known a Jesus who long antedated the Gospel Messiah and who presented to the student some one hundred and eight items of identity, similarity and correspondence in word, deed, and function with his later copy. (Alvin Boyd Kuhn, *Who Is This King of Glory?*, Elizabeth, N.J.: Academy Press, 1944, pp. x-xi.)

# Chapter X
# Gnosticism

Gnosticism flourished in Egypt and Western Asia between 250 B.C. and AD. 400. It was a Theosophic movement made up of elements of Egyptian mythology, Indian metaphysics, Judaism, and Greek philosophy. Gnosticism was overwhelmed by Christianity in the fourth century, AD., but some of the lost Gnostic literature has been recovered, and I shall briefly consider it. The ancient Gnostics were those who knew, just as the modern Agnostics are those who do not know. Gnostics believed in a Supreme God who was both unknown and unknowable. This unknown god was not the creator of the world; this task was delegated to lesser gods, who were emanations of the Supreme God. These subordinate gods, who created and governed the world, were called Aeons. Among the Aeons were the Logos (The Word), *Sophia* (Wisdom), Nous (Mind), *Phronesis* (Judgment), and *Dynamis* (Power); all attributes of the Supreme God, but existing separately. The Supreme God and the Aeons altogether formed the *Pleroma* (Fullness of the Godhead). In the Gospel of St. John, the Logos, or Word, is identified with the Christ. The Gnostic influence among the primitive Christians was very strong. St. Paul, the apostle to the Gentiles, was Gnostic. As Rhys has observed:

> It will be noticed that generally speaking the earlier Epistles show signs of Gnostic influence, while the later show signs of anti-Gnostic bias. In the earlier, Christ is spoken of as a spiritual being who has always existed. . . . This Christ spirit was in Paul himself, just as it had been in Jesus: "Christ liveth in me." (Galatians 2:20) *(Shaken Creeds*, p. 39.) A later Christian Gnostic, Manes (216-275), formed a sect known as the Manichaeans. The Manichaeans according to Rhys, "believed that Jesus descended from heaven in the form of a man about thirty years of age. His body was illusory, as he was in reality a purely spiritual being; and in the same way the dove (Holy Spirit) which descended upon him, or rather into him, at his baptism was also an illusion." Manes, the founder of this sect, described the Virgin Birth story as a fable which had grown up around the imaginary figure of this pre-existing spirit Jesus, and drew at-

tention to the fact that no first-hand witness gave evidence to its occurrence. (Rhys, *Shaken Creeds,* p. 173.)

A later form of Manichaean Gnosticism was established in the late sixth century of Mazdak, who combined his religious doctrine with socialism: Mazdakism is mentioned in Chapter XLI of Gibbon's *Decline and Fall of the Roman Empire,* and Professor J. B. Bury appended the following note on this esoteric cult:

> Its religious character distinguished Mazdakism from all modern socialistic theories. His doctrines were embraced by the ancient Gnostics and Mazdak was enrolled by them with Thoth, Saturn, Zoroaster, Pythagoras, Epicurus, John and Christ as teachers of the true Gnostic doctrines. (Gibbon, *History of the Decline and Fall* of the *Roman Empire,* ed. by Oliphant Smeaton, Vol. II, Modern Library Two-Volume Edition, pp. 255-256.)

Readers who wish more intelligence on Gnosticism should consult some of the works of G. R. S. Mead. For beginners, we recommend *Fragments of a Faith Forgotten* (New Hyde Park, NY: University Books, 1960). For those with a background knowledge of comparative religion, it would be advisable to consult three books by G. R. S. Mead, *Pistis Sophia, A Gnostic Gospel* (Secaucus, NJ: University Books, Inc., 1974), *Did Jesus Live 100 B. C.?,* (New Hyde Park, N.Y: University Books, 1960), and *Thrice Greatest Hermes* (London and Benares, 1906; reprinted in 3 vols. London: John M. Watkins, 1949).

After the Roman Emperor Constantine made the Christian religion the State religion of the empire, the remaining Gnostics were persecuted out of existence and their literature was destroyed. How and why Gnosticism was destroyed by organized Christianity is, as a rule, glossed over in history textbooks. One American scholar has penned an accurate and colorful account of these episodes:

> Preceding Christianity there was a school of science and philosophy which had accumulated practically all the wisdom and knowledge understandable to mankind. The object was to broadly educate the masses of the people by a unit system which would give to humanity a wisdom in common. This was the most potential period in human intellectual advancement

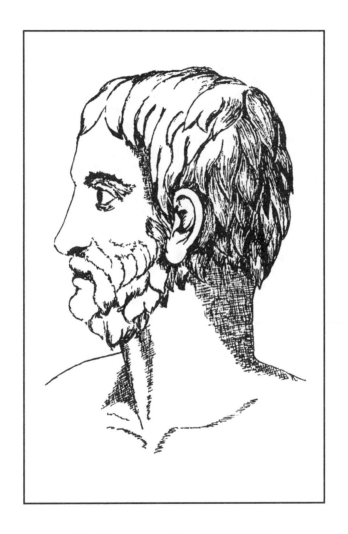

**Pythagoras (b. 582 B.C.?)**

the world has known. This school was called Gnosticism. Gnosis means to know — knowledge. Christianity means to believe — ignorance. These are the two schools; the one advocating the universal education of men, the other the universal ignorance of men. The one desired to develop the unit man, the other desired to suppress the unit and level all mankind to a common plastic mass. To accomplish this necessitated the suppressing of all extant knowledge; the closing of all the avenues through which people might acquire independent learning, education and intellectual training, and the debasement of humanity in abject ignorance . . .

The school which pitted itself against Gnosticism assumed the name *Ecclesia*. This name at once identified the purpose for which the organization was created to seize control of government, that it might exploit mankind for profit, and for its own glorification. Temporal power was the church goal. The name *Ecclesia* was derived from the Greek, and signified the legislative body which governed ancient Athens long before Christianity was invented. The first essential act of the Ecclesiasts was to suppress Gnosticism, and confiscate its vast accumulation of wisdom and knowledge, in order to control the education of future generations in a manner to adjust mankind to its purposes. Therefore the Gnostic wisdom was not wholly lost to the world but its great, universal educational system was supplanted. It is a well-established historical fact, not denied by the church that it required about 500 years to accomplish this submersion of Gnosticism, and to degrade the new generations in ignorance equal to the state of imbecility. History again points its accusing finger at the living evidence. The horrible results of such a crime against nature and mankind are pictured in the Dark Ages . . . Not even priests or prelates were permitted to learn to read or write. Even bishops could barely spell out their Latin. During this period of mental darkness, the ignorant masses were trained in intolerance, bigotry, fanaticism, and superstitious fear of an invisible power secretly controlled by the church; all of which begat a state of hysteria and imbecility. Through this terrorism popes seized control of the temporal power, retaining this control for nearly 500 years. They appointed and deposed kings at will, hence they dictated legislation to their ends and purposes — the very essence of government . . . This process of legislating evil into mankind is to vindicate that damnable doctrine of original sin, which slanders nature and insults all mankind . . . Originally the motive was to confiscate the intellects of man, but the modern policy is much more concerned in confiscating their personal rights and property. Here is the other aspect of the suppression of Gnosticism. Its method of teaching was an understandable symbolism. It specifically recognized nature as the great teacher, and visible things as the traditional records of past events, in progressive evolution from the lowest state to the highest, with thinking, reasoning man as the highest evoluted being. Man did not fall, he was raised up by a natural promotion. Hence every man was a Gnostic to the extent of his accumulated knowledge and understanding. Thus each unit man became a teacher, and all men were given equal rights in the acquirement of knowledge. It was wholly an educational system, and a natural consequence in evolution. The Ecclesiasts being thoroughly familiar with the Gnostic wisdom concerning astronomy, chemistry, and mathematics, as demonstrated by the splendid systems of Babylon, Egypt and Assyria, conceived the idea of developing a religio-political form of universal government, to control and exploit the future generations of people upon the earth through living, personified agents of the imaginary heavenly powers . . . to monopolize such a divine power as that contemplated it was necessary to personify nature, using the Gnostic system of symbolisms, and to give to these wholly imaginary beings names and functions. The Gnostic system had to be confiscated, and Gnosticism suppressed, to prevent exposure. This is why Christianity is so viciously antagonistic towards science and philosophy. (Thomas Sawyer Spivey, . *The Last of The Gnostic Masters*, Beverly Hills, California: Published by the author, 1926, pp. 544-551.)

In addition to the sources and authorities listed above, I recommend also Dr. Alvin Boyd Kuhn, *Shadow of the Third Century.*

# Chapter XI
# The Myth Theory of Christian Origins

Two principal types of Savior-Gods have been recognized by hierologists: vegetation gods and astral gods. The vegetation theory was presented with great erudition by Sir James G . Frazer in *The Golden Bough,* Abridged Edition (New York: The Macmillan Co., 1949), and also by Grant Allen in *The Evolution of The Idea of God* (London, Watts and Co., 1931). The stellar, lunar and solar myth theories have been treated with vast scholarship by Charles F. Dupuis, Count Volney, Gerald Massey, Dr. Albert Churchward, Dr. Alvin Boyd Kuhn, John M. Robertson, Godfrey Higgins, Ernest Busenbark, and Rev. Robert Taylor. Other experts will be cited as I proceed, but the men named above are among the outstanding authorities. An accurate and concise summary of the vegetation theory has been given by Dr. Forsyth:

> Many gods besides Christ have been supposed to die, be resurrected and ascend to heaven. This idea has now been traced back to its origin among primitive people in the annual death and resurrection of crops and plant life generally. This explains the world-wide prevalence of the notion. Among still more primitive tribes, Grant Allen showed, it is not yet understood that sown corn sprouts because of the spring sunshine, and they attribute the result to divine agency. To this end, they are accustomed at seed time to kill their tribal god — either in human or animal form — and scatter the flesh and the blood over the sown fields. They believe that the seeds will not grow unless the god is sacrificed and added to them in this manner. When, therefore, the crop appears, they never doubt that it is their god coming to life again. It is from this erroneous belief of primitive tribes that Christianity today derives its belief in Christ's death and resurrection. (David Forsyth, *Psychology and Religion,* London: Watts and Company, 1935, p. 97.)

The specialists in solar mythology have regarded the ancient crucified Saviors as personifications of the sun and believed that their biographies were allegories of the sun's passage through the twelve constellations of the zodiac. This theory has been oversimplified by some scholars, since stellar and lunar elements also enter into the solar mythology. The vegetation cults were the most ancient, but they were later blended with the astral worship. In the primitive sacrificial rites, the victim was originally the king or chief of the tribe or clan. The prosperity of the group was supposed to have a magical relation to the health of the king. If the ruler became old and feeble, it was thought that the nation or tribe would suffer a similar decline, so the king, considered to be a god in human form, was sacrificed for the good of all and then replaced with a younger and more vigorous successor. In later times the king's son was chosen as the scapegoat, and, being of divine origin, was called the son of the god. In even later days a condemned criminal replaced the royal victim. The culprit was given regal honors for a time, then put to death. He was usually slain while bound to a tree with arms outstretched, as if on a cross. After being entombed, he was believed to rise from the dead within three days; the three-day period being based on the three-day interval between the old and new moons. Berossus in his Chaldean History tells of an annual festival celebrated in Babylonia, called the *Sacaea*. This fete lasted five days, and during that time masters and servants exchanged places in society. The king temporarily gave up his throne, and a mock king, Zoganes, took his place. After five days the mock king was dethroned, scourged, and then either hanged or crucified. "In this regard," an eminent Egyptologist remarked, "it is interesting to notice that in the Acts, the writer mistakenly speaks of Jesus as having been slain and then hanged to a tree, as though this were a common phrase coming readily to his mind, and the word *hanged* is frequently used in Greek to denote crucifixion." (Weigall, *The Paganism in our Christianity,* pp. 77-78.)

The Roman scholar Macrobius (fourth century) in his *Saturnalia* discussed the practice in pagan temples of representing the gods at different ages of their lives and stated that:

> These differences of age refer to the sun which seems to be a babe at the Winter Solstice (Christmas), as the Egyptians represent him in their temples on a certain day; that being the shortest day, he is then supposed to be small and an infant.

This hypothesis was not original with Macrobius, who in all probability obtained it from the priests of Egypt. In Egypt, 3000 years ago, the birthdate of the sun-god was celebrated on the 25th of December; the first day to noticeably lengthen after the day of the Winter Solstice (the 21st of December). At the midnight hour on the first minutes of the 25th of December the birthday of the sun was commemorated. The sun was then in the zodiacal sign of Capricorn, then known as the Stable of Augeus, so the infant sun-god was said to have been born in a stable. Brightly shining on the meridian was Sirius (The Star from the East); while rising in the east was Virgo (The Virgin), with the horizon passing through the center of the constellation. To the right of Sirius was the constellation Orion (The Great Hunter), with three stars in his belt. These stars, in a straight line, point at Sirius and were anciently known as the "three kings." We have met them in the Gospels as the three Magi or wise men from the East. In the Zodiac of Denderah the constellation Virgo was pictured as a woman with a spike of corn in one hand, and on the adjacent margin the Virgin was denoted by a figure of Isis with Horus in her arms. If anyone doubts the relevance of this to the Christian cult, then ponder the words of Edward Carpenter:

> But it is well known as a matter of history that the worship of Isis and Horus descended in the early Christian centuries to Alexandria, where it took the form of the worship of the Virgin Mary and the infant Savior and so passed into the European ceremonial. We have therefore the Virgin Mary connected by linear succession and descent with that remote Zodiacal cluster in the sky! . . . A curious confirmation of the same astronomical connection is afforded by the Roman Catholic Calendar. For if this be consulted, it will be found that the festival of the Assumption of the Virgin is placed on the 15th August, while the festival of the birth of the Virgin is dated the 8th September. . . . At the present day, the Zodiacal signs (owing to precession) have shifted some distance from the constellations of the same name. But at the time when the Zodiac was constituted and these names were given, the first date obviously would signalize the actual disappearance of the cluster *Virgo* in the sun's rays — i.e., the Assumption of the Virgin into the glory of the God — while the second date would signalize the reappearance of the constellation or the Birth of the Virgin. (Edward Carpenter, *Pagan and Christian Creeds*, New York: Harcourt, Brace and Co., 1920, pp. 32-33.)

At the Winter Solstice the sun was at the lowest point of the celestial sphere, at its southern limits, then it began to move northward along the ecliptic passing over the celestial equator at the Vernal Equinox (Easter). The crossing of the sun from the south to the north side of the equator was the origin of the festival of the Passover. When the sun passed over the celestial equator 3000 years ago it was situated in Aries the Lamb, or Ram, so the lamb became the symbol of the sun-god. This suggests the origin of the Paschal Lamb, widely known as a symbol of the crucified Christ. Several of the sacrificed saviors were said to have been crucified in the heavens. This solar crucifixion may be explained as follows:

> For in an astronomical chart, the sun is apparently crucified upon the intersecting lines of the Equator and the Ecliptic at the moment of his descent into the lower hemisphere, the hemisphere of darkness and death; and so again at the moment of his resurrection into the hemisphere of light and life, while the period of transit is three days. At the time when the myth of the death of the sun-god originated, the sun, being in the constellation Aries at the Spring Equinox, was identified with the Ram. That is the Lamb which has been slain from the foundation of the world. The custom of dressing the paschal lamb in the shape of a cross is referable to the same myth. (L. Gordon Rylands, *The Beginnings of Gnostic Christianity*, London: Watts and Co., 1940, p. 217.)

In the vast corpus of world mythology we have vegetation gods, tree gods, star gods, moon gods, sun gods, etc., but Osiris of Egypt seems to have been all of these blended into one. In the Temple of Isis at Philae was an engraving of the body of Osiris with stalks of corn growing out of it, and sometimes this god was called the crop or harvest, so he was symbolic of the corn which annually died and came to life again. Besides being a corn spirit, Osiris was also a tree god. His worshippers chopped down a pine tree and hollowed out the center. An image of Osiris was fashioned from the excavated wood and buried like a corpse in the hollow of a tree. The image was kept for a year and then burned in the Hall of Osiris at Denderah. There is a picture of a coffin enclosed within the trunk of a tree, and in the coffin is the hawk-headed mummy of the god.

Osiris was, in addition, a god of fertility, for phallic images of him were shown in the temples and carried in processions. To cite Frazer:

As a god of vegetation Osiris was naturally conceived as a god of creative energy in general, since
men at a certain stage of evolution fail to distinguish
between the reproductive powers of animals and of
plants . . . At his festival women used to go about the
villages singing songs in his praise and carrying
obscene images of him which they set in motion by
means of strings. The custom was probably a charm to
ensure the growth of crops. (Frazer, *The Golden
Bough*, Abridged Edition, p. 381.)

Osiris, in one aspect, was a god of the dead. Among his titles
were: Ruler of the Dead, Lord of the Underworld, and Lord of
Eternity. On the monument he occupies the judgment seat and
holds the staff of authority and the cross of life. On his breast a St.
Andrews cross may be seen, and his throne is covered with a pat-
tern of squares in two colors, like a chessboard, representing the
good and evil which he was required to judge.

That Osiris shone as a moon-god we are not permitted to doubt.
Osiris is credited with ruling over Egypt for twenty-eight years.
This is symbolic of the twenty-eight days of the lunar month. The
rending of the corpse of Osiris into fourteen parts by Set and his fellow conspirators refers to the waning of the moon, which was imagined to lose a part of itself on each of the fourteen days of the second half of the lunar month. The mythical account tells of Set's discovery of the body of Osiris at the time of the full moon, so the dis-
memberment took place during the waning of the moon. An explanation of this was given by Gerald Massey:

Osiris as light giver in the moon was torn in fourteen pieces during the latter half of the lunation by
the evil Sut, the opposing power of darkness. He was
put together again and reconstituted by his son,
beloved Horus, the young solar god. This representation could not have been made until it was known
that the lunar light was replenished monthly from
the solar source. Then Horus as the sun-god and the
vanquisher of Sut, the power of darkness, could be
called the reconstitutor of Osiris in the moon. (Gerald
Massey, *Ancient Egypt*, Vol. I, p. 187.)

The spring season in Egypt was heralded by the new moon of the
month of Phamenoth, and at this time in the temples the ceremony
of the entry of Osiris into the moon was celebrated. At the rite of

the burial of Osiris, his worshippers built a crescent-shaped chest, because the moon approaching the sun becomes crescent-shaped and then vanishes. On the monuments Osiris is sometimes seen as a human-headed mummy, holding the emblems of power, and wearing on his head the image of a full moon within a crescent.

The role of Osiris as a sun-god is beyond all dispute among the knowledgeable. The only authority that dogmatically denied this was Sir J. G. Frazer, who argued that since Osiris was a god of vegetation, then he could not have been a sun-god. (*The Golden Bough,* Abridged Edition, p. 384.) This brought a sharp retort from the Right Honorable John M. Robertson:

> Rightly intent on establishing a hitherto ill-developed principle of mythological interpretation, the cult of the vegetation spirit, Dr. Frazer had unduly ignored the conjunction seen deductively to be inevitable, and inductively to be normal, between the concept of the vegetation god and that of others, in particular the sun-god. He becomes for once vigorously polemical in his attack on the thesis that Osiris was a sun-god, as if that were excluded once for all by proving him a vegetation god. The answer is that he was both, and that such a synthesis was inevitable . . . Dionysus and Adonis, Dr. Frazer shows, are vegetation gods. Yet they too are both born on December 25th, as was the Babe Sun-god Horus, who however was exhibited as rising from a lotus plant. Now, why should the vegetation god be born at the winter solstice save as having been identified with the sun-god? (John M. Robertson, *Christianity and Mythology,* p. 33.)

The esoteric religious rites of the ancient Egyptians were known as the MYSTERIES. There were two sets of Mysteries. Osiris was the god of the Greater Mysteries, and Isis was worshipped in the Lesser Mysteries. The Mysteries were based on dramatic performances representing the death of Osiris (the sun-god) and the search for his body by Isis (the moon goddess). Many ancient nations celebrated mysteries, but those of Egypt were the earliest. In the words of Brown:

> The mysteries of all the other nations were quite similar to those of Egypt, and were no doubt derived from them. (Robert Brown, Jr., *Stellar Theology and*

*Masonic Astronomy*, New York: D. Appleton and Co., 1882, p. 11.)

The sacerdotal caste of ancient Egypt were an admirable group of men, possessed of keen intellect, profound knowledge, and high character. The Mystery Schools of Egypt were the world's earliest universities. The wise men of ancient Greece went to Egypt for their higher education. Among these men were Plato, Thales, Eudoxus, and Pythagoras. Plato studied in the Nile Valley for thirteen years. The metaphysical doctrines now called Platonic were first taught in the sanctuaries of Thebes, Memphis, and Heliopolis long before Plato was born. The literature of the Egyptian Mysteries is not extensive, but there are some surviving fragments which we can study with profit. Iamblicus, a Greek philosopher of the fourth century, wrote a learned treatise on *The Mysteries of the Egyptians* (see Paul Christian, *The History and Practice* of *Magic*, 2 Vols. New York: The Citadel Press, 1969, especially Book Two, Chapters I-V, pp. 81-126) in which he described some of the tests faced by candidates for membership in that secret order.

When a postulant applied for admission to the sacred brotherhood, he was greeted by two *Thesmothetes* (Guardians of the Rites). The ceremony took place at night, and the applicant, with bandaged eyes, was led to the entrance of the temple. After entering the sacred precincts the postulant was led down a spiral staircase of twenty-two steps, and there a door was opened which gave access to a circular room. The candidate was then told that he was on the brink of a precipice. "This abyss," said the guide, "surrounds the Temple of the Mysteries, and protects it against the temerity and curiosity of the profane. We have arrived a little too soon; our brethren have not lowered the drawbridge by which the initiates communicate with the sacred place. Let us wait for their arrival, but, if you value your life, do not move; cross your hands on your breast, and do not take off the bandage until the signal is given." The postulate, of course, obeyed, and the Thesmothetes then took from an altar robes of linen, a gold and a silver belt, and two masks —one of a lion's head, the other, that of a bull. The robes were emblems of moral purity. The gold belt was consecrated to the Sun; the silver one to the Moon. The lion's head symbolized the zodiacal sign Leo, the throne of the genius of the Sun; the bull's head symbolized the sign of Taurus, the throne of the genius of the Moon. After the Thesmothetes donned their masks, a trap door opened in the floor with a clanging sound, and from this opening a mechanical monster arose brandishing a scythe and loudly cried: "Woe to him who comes to disturb the peace of the dead!" At this point the eyes of the postulant were unbandaged, and he found himself facing the monster. The spectre with the scythe brushed his head seven times with that implement, then vanished as the trap door closed with a bang. If the postulant had not by this time collapsed from fright, the Thesmothetes then removed their beast-like masks and commended him for his courage, saying: "You felt the chill of murderous steel and you did not recoil; you looked at the horror of horrors and your eyes defied it; well done. But among us there is a virtue higher than manly courage, and that is the voluntary humility which triumphs over the vanity of pride. Are you capable of such a victory over yourself?" After giving assent, the candidate faced another test. "Very well," he was told, "will you crawl flat on the ground, right to the innermost sanctuary, where our brethren await you, to give you knowledge and power in exchange for humility?" The postulant again signified assent and was given the following command: "Then take this lamp; it is the image of God's face, when we walk hidden from the sight of men. Go without fear; you have only yourself to be afraid of in the test of solitude." One of the guides next touched a hidden spring in the wall which caused an iron plaque to slide sideways, revealing a long and narrow tunnel. Then the candidate was told: "Let this path be for you the image of the tomb, in which all men find their rest in the evening of life: yet only to awake freed from the darkness of material things in the eternal dawn of life in the spirit. You have vanquished the spectre of death; go triumph over the horrors of the tomb." On entering the tunnel . . the admitting door clanged to a close behind the pilgrim, and a voice in the distance said: "Here perish all fools who covet knowledge and power!" This message was transmitted acoustically, fading away through seven distinctly spaced echoes. Finally, the struggling postulant emerged from the tunnel; above him was a rising roof, in front of him a downward sloping path, and at last a dark pit was reached, on the brink of which was an iron ladder descending into the depths. After climbing down seventy-eight rungs of the ladder to its termination, the potential initiate could see no bottom to the pit, so then he climbed back upward and with lamp in hand found a crevice and, passing into it, discovered a spiral stairway. After climbing twenty-two steps up the stairs, the postulant saw through a bronze grating a long-gallery flanked by two rows of sculptured Sphinxes, twenty-four in number, twelve on each side. Between the statues the walls were covered with frescoes showing mysterious personages and symbols. There were altogether twenty-two pictures, eleven on each side, facing each other, and the gallery was illuminated by lamps situated on eleven bronze tripods with wicks fueled by aromatic oils.

**Plato (427-347 B.C.)**

**Thales (640-550 B.C.)**

At this point a Magus, known as a Pastophore (Guardian of the Sacred Symbols), opened the grating to the entrance of the gallery and said to the awaiting postulant: "Son of Earth, be welcome! You have escaped the pit by discovering the path of wisdom. Few aspirants to the Mysteries have triumphed over this test; the others have all perished. Since the great Isis is your protector, she will lead you, I hope, safe and sound to the sanctuary, where virtue receives its crown. I must not hide from you that other perils lie in store; but I am allowed to encourage you by explaining these symbols, the understanding of which creates for the heart of man an invincible armor. Come with me and contemplate these sacred images; listen carefully to my words, and, if you can mind them in your memory, the kings of the world will be less powerful than you when you return to earth."

The Pastophore pointed out the paintings to the postulant one at a time, but before going into details, explained the general meaning of the twenty-two *Arcana,* as these frescoes were called, as follows:

> The Science of Will, the principle of all wisdom, and source of all power is contained in twenty-two Arcana, or symbolic hieroglyphs, each of whose attributes conceals a certain meaning, and which, taken as a whole, compose an absolute doctrine, memorized by its correspondence with the Letters of the sacred language, and with the numbers that are connected with these Letters. Each Letter and each Number, contemplated by the eye, or uttered by the mouth, expresses a reality of the *divine world,* the *intellectual world,* and the *physical world.* Each arcanum, made visible or tangible by one of these paintings, is a formula, of a law of human activity, in its relations with spiritual and material forces, whose combination produces the phenomena of life.

The twenty-two Arcana are described below:

### Arcanum One
**Letter A**       **Number 1**

> This fresco featured the picture of the Magus, or the Wise man. He wore a fine robe, and his belt was made in the form of a serpent biting its own tail (a symbol of eternity). He wore a golden headdress, symbolic of the light of the sun. In his right hand was a scepter of

**Sphinx**

gold, the image of command, raised heavenward as a gesture of aspiration toward knowledge, wisdom, and power. The index finger of the left hand pointed to the ground, signifying~that the mission of the perfect man was to reign over the material world. Before the Magus, on a square stone, were depicted a goblet, a sword, and a gold coin embellished with a cross. The goblet stood for the mixture of passion producing happiness or misery. The sword represented the strivings leading to the conquest of obstacles. The gold coin symbolized worthwhile achievements, and the cross engraved on the coin was emblematic of the power to be attained in the world of the future.

### Arcanum Two
### Letter B        Number 2

Here was the picture of a woman seated on the threshold of a Temple of Isis and on her head was a crown topped by a crescent moon. Her face was veiled, a solar cross on her breast, and in her lap an open book, half-covered by a cloak. The seated woman symbolized Occult Science waiting for the initiate on the threshold of the Temple of Isis. The solar cross stood for Matter energized by Spirit; the veil was an emblem of Truth, hiding itself from profane curiosity, and the half-hidden book meant that the Mysteries were revealed only to the wise man who wrapped himself in the cloak of silent meditation.

### Arcanum Three
### Letter C        Number 3

The feature here was a woman seated at the center of a blazing sun crowned by twelve stars and with her feet resting on the moon. The woman was the symbol of Mother Nature; the sun represented creative strength; the twelve stars stood for the twelve signs of the Zodiac, and the Moon signified Matter and its domination by Spirit.

## Arcanum Four
### Letter D      Number 4

This painting was that of a man seated on a square stone holding a scepter, while on his head was a helmet topped by a crown. The stone cube stood for conquered matter; the scepter was a symbol of the goddess Isis; and the crowned helmet signified strength conquering power.

## Arcanum Five
### Letter E      Number 5

This fresco featured the Hierophant (Master of the Sacred Mysteries) and represented the Genius of Good Intentions and the Spirit of Conscience.

## Arcanum Six
### Letters U, V      Number 6

Here was shown a man standing at a crossroads flanked by two women, each woman with a hand on the man's shoulder and with each of the other hands pointing to one of two roads. The woman on the right, with a golden headdress, represented Virtue; the one on the left, crowned with vine leaves, depicted Vice.

## Arcanum Seven
### Letter Z      Number 7

This picture was that of a conqueror riding in a chariot with a sword in one hand and a scepter in the other. The sword was a sign of victory; the scepter, embellished with a triangle, symbolized Spirit. A square (standing for Matter) and a circle (signifying Eternity) altogether represented the dominance of Mind over Matter.

## Arcanum Eight
### Letter H      Number 8

This Arcanum showed a woman on a throne holding in one hand an upward pointing sword and with the other a pair of scales, symbolic of Justice opposing Evil with a sword and weighing the deeds of mankind in a balance.

### Arcanum Nine
### Letters T, H     Number 9

This fresco was that of an old man walking and leaning on a stick and holding in front of himself a lantern, half hidden by a cloak. The old man represented Experience acquired in the labors of life; the light of the lantern was the Mind, which illuminated past, present, and future; the concealing cloak was Discretion; and the stick symbolized Prudence.

### Arcanum Ten
### Letters I, J, Y     Number 10

A wheel was here shown suspended on its axle between two columns. This was the Wheel of Fate. On the right, Hermanubis, the Good Spirit, was shown climbing to the top of the wheel. On the left, Set, the Evil Spirit, was depicted as being cast down. A Sphinx, balanced on top of the wheel, held a sword in his leonine paws, which represented destiny, ready to strike to right or left. The turning wheel caused the humble to rise and the mighty to be cast down.

### Arcanum 11
### Letters C, K     Number 20

Here was pictured the image of a maiden closing the jaws of a lion with her bare hands, and this was symbolic of the strength created by self-confidence.

### Arcanum Twelve
### Letter L     Number 30

This fresco showed a man hanging by one foot from a gallows; the sign of a violent death brought on by a tragic accident.

### Arcanum Thirteen
#### Letter M          Number 40

In a meadow was shown a skeleton cutting off the heads of men, while on the ground the hands and feet of men sprouted up. This signified the rebirth of all forms of Being in the realm of Time.

### Arcanum Fourteen
#### Letter N          Number 50

Here we have the Spirit of the Sun holding two urns and pouring from one into the other the sap of life; this symbolizing the various combinations produced by Nature.

### Arcanum Fifteen
#### Letter X          Number 60

This scene featured Set, the Spirit of Evil, rising out of a flaming abyss and holding a torch above two men chained at his feet. This was the symbol of Fatality which overwhelmed great or small, strong or weak.

### Arcanum Sixteen
#### Letter O          Number 70

A tower is shown being struck by lightning, and a crowned and an uncrowned man being cast down from its summit; this being symbolic of material forces which crush both the great and the small alike.

### Arcanum Seventeen
#### Letters F, P          Number 80

A picture of a blazing star with eight rays surrounded by seven other stars. This was the Star of Destiny. The seven other stars represented the Sun, the Moon, and the five planets visible to the naked eye.

### Arcanum Eighteen
#### Letters T, S     Number 90

Here we see a tower in the midst of a barren landscape with a path on each side and illuminated by a half-clouded Moon at twilight. This depicted a false security which did not see hidden perils.

### Arcanum Nineteen
#### Letter Q     Number 100

A radiant Sun was shown shining on two small children holding hands in the midst of a circle of flowers, and this symbolized the happiness of a simple life.

### Arcanum Twenty
#### Letter R     Number 200

This picture was of a Spirit blowing a trumpet over a half-opened tomb from which a man, woman, and child were rising. This was a sign of change, of the end of all things both Good and Evil.

### Arcanum Twenty-One
#### Letter S     Number 300

A picture of a blind man with a bulging wallet about to collide with a broken obelisk on which was a crocodile with open jaws. The blind man represented a slave of material things, and his wallet was filled with Errors and Faults. The obelisk represented the ruin of his works, and the crocodile was an emblem of Fate.

### Arcanum Twenty-Two
#### Letter T     Number 400

Here was a Star surrounded by a garland of roses arranged to form a circle. At the four quarters of the circle were, respectively, the heads of a Man, a Bull, a Lion, and an Eagle. These symbols corresponded to the four quarter signs of the Zodiac: Aquarius, Taurus, Leo, and Scorpio.

At the end of the gallery of the Arcana the Pastophore opened a door and showed the postulant a long narrow vault, at the end of which was a blazing furnace, then said to him:

Son of Earth, death itself frightens the imperfect only. If you are afraid, what are you doing here? Look at me; once I too passed through those flames as if they were a garden of roses.

The postulant then walked toward the flames and found them to be an optical illusion produced by lights. He then walked on and came to a pool, and on looking back saw flaming oil falling from a hole in the ceiling. So he was between the ordeals of fire and water and proceeded to walk into the pool. At the middle of the pool the water was neck-high, but he kept going and the slope of the pool began to rise as he walked on to the other side of the water. There, after ascending a flight of steps, he reached a platform surrounded on three sides by a lofty arcade. Locating a door on a wall and opening aforesaid door, a voice was heard saying: "If you stop you will perish, behind you is death; before you, salvation." On the door was a ring, which when grasped by the postulant, caused the floor to collapse under him, leaving him hanging over a pit. As he held on to the ring the floor came back under his feet, and the door opened. Inside the door he was met by a delegation of twelve Neocores (Guardians of the Sanctuary). The eyes of the postulant were then bandaged, and he was led through another tunnel. Afterwards the party passed through several secret doors by giving passwords and signs of recognition. In an underground vault the College of the Magi awaited the arrival of the new applicant. On the platform was the Hierophant, clad in a purple robe; on his head was a golden circlet decorated with the images of seven stars, and this dignitary sat on a silver throne. The other Magi, wearing albs and plain gold circlets on their heads, were seated in a triple semicircle around the Hierophant, but on a lower level. Escorted by the twelve Neocores, the postulant was led into the assemblage of the Magi. The new candidate was greeted by the Hierophant, who requested him to make a solemn vow never to reveal anything seen or heard in the initiation ceremonies. The postulant then knelt at the altar and gave the necessary oath. He was then informed by the Hierophant that:

From this hour forward you are counted among the number of the disciples of Wisdom, and you will bear among us the title of Zealot, until by some great act of obedience and self-abnegation, you have deserved to be raised to a higher rank.

The new initiate was then required to make a second oath, swearing obedience to the Hierophant, which he did. After this the bandage was removed, and the neophyte saw all the Magi pointing swords at his breast. Again the Hierophant spoke:

These swords symbolize human justice, but this often is fallible or slow, and the fear it inspires does not stop man's audacity. We want heaven itself to guarantee the faith of the new initiates. You have sworn me absolute obedience; you must test it by an ordeal from which only the all-powerful can save you; if he judge you worthy of life.

The swords were then lowered. Then two Neocores approached, each carrying a goblet. "You see these goblets," declared the Hierophant, "the contents of one is harmless; in the other is a violent poison. I command you to seize without reflection one of them and empty it in a single draught." This order was obeyed by the candidate, who was relieved to find no harmful results ensuing. He was then informed that he was in no danger, since the contents of both goblets were harmless. After passing other tests successfully, the postulant was finally accepted into membership in the Mysteries. Then he was permitted to join the Magi in a religious banquet.

After becoming a Zealot, if the new initiate sought promotion to a higher rank, he had to study twelve more years with the Magi. The next grade, the second, was that of the *Theoricus*. The third grade bore the name *Practicus*. A fourth grade initiate was called a Philosopher. The fifth grade title was Minor Adept; the sixth grade, Major Adept; the seventh, Franchised Adept; and the eighth, Master of the Temple. Finally, the ninth grade initiate was called Magus of the Rose-Cross. Only the Magi of the ninth Degree were permitted to govern the state.

The Savior-God religions, Christianity included, are based on the Worship of nature. Nature may be defined as the material universe and the forces at work in the cosmos, which operate independently of man. Among the many varieties of natural religion were: the worship of the earth, of trees, and other plants; of volcanoes, mountains, water, and wind; of animals; of stars, planets, the moon, the sun, the sky, etc. This nature worship was based on the doctrine of

Animism; a belief that material objects are inhabited by indwelling spiritual forces. This doctrine evolved through three stages:

1. The conception of human souls or spirits.
2. A belief in non-human spirits regarded as the cause of natural events.
3. The belief in gods, one or many.

The earliest important religious cult was the worship of the earth in the image of the Great Mother. Mother Earth was the first great terrestrial deity. Among other terrestrial cults were the worship of plants and animals. At a later date Sky Worship developed, and Father Sky became the consort of Mother Earth. The general worship of the sky evolved in due time into the following celestial cults:

1. Star and Planet Worship
2. Moon Worship
3. Sun Worship

Later on in time these various cults intermixed and blended and became quite complex. In the mythology of ancient Egypt the various gods were closely associated with the calendar. Stars were used to measure time in Egypt and Western Asia as early as 14,500 B.C. Later on, a lunar calendar was developed, and finally, a solar calendar. When you combine the stars, the moon, the planets, and the sun in an endeavor to tell time accurately, the understanding of the complete system requires considerable study. For instance, in the study of the astral theology of Ancient Egypt, as an eminent authority pointed out:

> The casual reader would be at a loss to know which was the supreme god of the Egyptians — whether Ra, Osiris or Horus . . . Ra is the Sun-god, the god of the solar-year; Osiris is god of the luni-solar year of 364 days, and merges in Ra when the year is reconstituted, to be of proper length; and Horus represents the added part, and thus the accurate year..
>
> (St. Clair, *Creation Records,* p. 343.)

Temples were erected in Upper Egypt about 6400 B.C., oriented to the star Canopus, which symbolized Khonsu, an early southern star god. The ancient Egyptians worshipped two sets of polar gods, both eight in number, and four compass gods. The eight polar gods of the north were ultimately combined with the four compass gods to make up the twelve zodiacal gods. There were two types of zodiac: lunar and solar. The lunar zodiac, with its twenty-seven or twenty-eight lunar mansions, was much earlier than the solar zodiac with its twelve signs. Since civilization in Africa originated south of the equator, the earliest Nilotic polar gods were those relating to the South Pole. Khnumu was the God of the South Pole. He was the Creator of the Universe and the maker of man. He was called the Lord of Nubia and was depicted as ram-headed. In his creative work he was assisted by seven architects. Ptah was the God of the North Pole. He was also a creator-god and was assisted by his seven sons. The seven architects of Khnumu and the seven sons of Ptah symbolized the seven positions of the changing pole stars due to the precession of the Equinoxes. There were, as a result, a total of eight gods at each pole, both North and South.

The original zodiac had only four constellations situated at the four corners of the sky; the position of the two Equinoxes and the two Solstices. The other eight were later fitted in between the original four. In ancient Egypt the names, symbols, directions, colors, and seasons were as listed:

| *Names* | *Symbols* | *Directions* | *Colors* | *Seasons* |
|---------|-----------|--------------|----------|-----------|
| Amset | Man | North | Red | Winter |
| Tuamutef | Jackal | East | White | Spring |
| Gebhsennuf | Hawk | West | White | Autumn |
| Hapi | Ape | South | Green | Summer |

These Compass gods, when later incorporated into the Zodiac, as standardized by the Greeks, were in respect to names, symbols, locations, and directions as here listed:

| *Names* | *Symbols* | *Locations* | *Directions* |
|---------|-----------|-------------|--------------|
| Aquarius | Waterman | Winter Solstice | North |
| Taurus | Bull | Vernal Equinox | East |
| Scorpio | Scorpion | Autumnal Equinox | West |
| Leo | Lion | Summer Solstice | South |

The original four zodiacal constellations and their principal stars were:

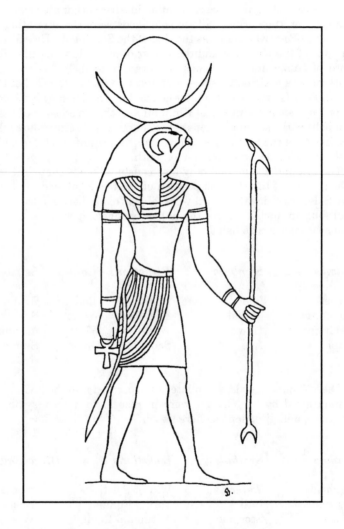

**Khonsu (Khensu or Khuns)**

| Stars | Constellations |
|-------|----------------|
| Regulus | Leo |
| Antares | Scorpio |
| Fomalhaut | Aquarius |
| Aldebaran | Taurus |

Among the ancient Hebrews, these symbols with their corresponding directions and seasons were:

| Names | Directions | Seasons |
|-------|-----------|---------|
| Man | North | Winter |
| Ox | East | Spring |
| Eagle | West | Autumn |
| Lion | South | Summer |

The early Christians adopted these symbols and related them to the four evangelists as follows:

| Names | Symbols | Directions | Seasons |
|-------|---------|-----------|---------|
| Matthew | Man | North | Winter |
| Luke | Ox | East | Spring |
| John | Eagle | West | Autumn |
| Mark | Lion | South | Summer |

A picture of the sculptured relief on Chartres Cathedral is shown on page 20, Carl G. Jung, *Man and His Symbols*, (Garden City, NY: Doubleday and Co., 1971) in which the four evangelists are depicted as follows:

> Mark as a Lion;
> Luke as an Ox;
> John as an Eagle; and
> Matthew as a Man.

On page 21 of the same book there is a picture of the four sons of Horus of Ancient Egypt. These are the four compass gods previously mentioned, and they were imagined as an Ape, Man, Jackal and Hawk. In both instances we have a group composed of three animals and one man.

This symbolism of the four quarters was known in both the Old and New Worlds in very remote ages. Among the Chaldeans of Western Asia these symbols were familiar, and their names, symbols, directions and seasons were:

| Names | Symbols | Directions | Seasons |
|---|---|---|---|
| Ustur | Man | North | Winter |
| Kirub | Bull | East | Spring |
| Natting | Eagle | West | Autumn |
| Nergal | Lion | South | Summer |

In Ancient China the compass gods were:
    (1) The Black Warrior of the North;
    (2) The Green Dragon of the East;
    (3) The White Tiger of the West; and
    (4) The Red Bird of the South.

In Ancient America this same complex prevailed among the Mayans and the Aztecs. Examples follow:

### Mayan

| Gods | Directions | Colors |
|---|---|---|
| Muluc | North | White |
| Kan | East | Red |
| Ix | West | Black |
| Cauac | South | Yellow |

### Aztec (Mexican)

| Gods | Directions | Colors |
|---|---|---|
| Tecpatl | North | White |
| Acatl | East | Red |
| Calli | West | Black |
| Tochtli | South | Yellow |

This symbolism of the Lords of the Four Quarters still survives in West Africa. In the words of Dr. Churchward:

> The people of Bivili, Bini, and Yoruba, West Africa, have the same under the names of
> (1) Ibara,
> (2) Edi,
> (3) Oyekun and
> (4) Oz-Be, and build these names, with Ifi, the Son of God, i.e., Horus — into the walls of their houses. (Churchward, *The Signs and Symbols of Primordial Man*, p. 320.)

The anthropologist, Lord Raglan, supplements the above with the following remarks:

> Turning to Africa, we are told that the Maligasi of Madagascar regard the cardinal points of the compass as four deities. On the mainland these beliefs seem to be confined to West Africa. Of the Ekoi of Nigeria . . . recent investigation has shown that the religious and ceremonial use of the number four has its origins in the recognition of four quarter-gods, and that a similar complex is found among the Igbo and Yoruba. And among the Songhai and Mande the world is considered to be divided into four quarters. The Igbo of Nigeria say that the earth was divided into four quarters by the crossing paths of the Sun and the Moon. (Lord Raglan, *The Temple and The House*, New York: W W Norton and Company, 1964, p. 165.)

Attentive readers of the Christian Bible will find many incidents of astral symbolism recorded in that work. In the Apocalypse we read about the four beasts, and the four horsemen; the beasts were the zodiacal constellations and the horsemen were the planets.
In Revelation 4:7 we read:

> The first beast *was* like a lion, and the second beast like a calf, and the third beast had a face as a man, and the fourth beast *was* like a flying eagle.

These celestial animals were the quarter constellations of the Zodiac of 5000 years ago. This fact was noticed and explained by Higgins, to wit:

The signs of the Zodiac, with the exception of the Scorpion, which was exchanged by Dan for the Eagle, were carried by the different tribes of the Israelites on their standards, and Taurus, Leo, Aquarius and Scorpio, or the Eagle, the four signs of Reuben, Judah, Ephraim and Dan, were placed at the four corners — the four cardinal points — of their encampment, evidently in allusion to the cardinal points of the sphere, the equinoxes and solstices, when the equinox was in Taurus. (Higgins, *Anacalypsis,* Vol. II, p. 105.)

As to the four horsemen and their steeds:

1. The first horseman was a conqueror armed with a bow, wearing a crown, and riding a white horse. This was the planet Venus.

2. The second horse was red, ridden by a warrior with a sword. This was the planet Mars.

3. The third horse was black with the rider holding aloft a pair of balances. This was the planet Saturn.

4. The fourth horse was of pale-green or blue-green color, and his rider was death.
   This was the planet Mercury.

There has been much speculation on the origin of the zodiac. One of the best was penned by George St. Clair:

About 6000 years ago, the spring sun would be entering Taurus; and the four quarter signs would be the Bull, the Lion, the Scorpion and the Waterman, though some of these signs might be otherwise named. In memory of that early arrangement — which in many ways left its mark — devises on rings were, for example, a scorpion, a lion, a hawk, and a cynocephalus ape ... From the four quarters we pass to the Twelve Signs. Between each two quarters signs two other signs were inserted. The planisphere of the temple of Denderah shows four gods supporting the heavens at the four quarter points corresponding to the Bull, the Lion, the Scorpion, and the Waterman; and shows eight other divinities in pairs, one on either side of each pillar, making up the twelve. (St. Clair, *Creation Records*, pp. 136-137.)

In the Biblical book of Genesis, Chapter 49, we may read the story of Jacob and his children, twelve sons and one daughter. A little study will show that Jacob was the Sun and that his children were the twelve zodiacal constellations. Arranged in their proper order they were:

| | | |
|---|---|---|
| Gad | — | Aries, |
| Issachar | — | Taurus, |
| Simeon and Levi | — | Gemini, |
| Benjamin | — | Cancer, |
| Judah | — | Leo, |
| Dinah | — | Virgo, |
| Asher | — | Libra, |
| Dan | — | Scorpio, |
| Joseph | — | Sagittarius, |
| Naphtali | — | Capricorn, |
| Reuben | — | Aquarius, and |
| Zebulon | — | Pisces. |

The zodiac with which we are familiar today originated with the Greeks, but there were earlier zodiacs with different symbols, going back to a remote antiquity. One of these was discussed by one of the great Egyptologists of the last century. I refer to Gerald Massey, whose six-volume study on the religion and mythology of ancient Egypt are certainly classics in their field of study. The following passage is from Massey's last and greatest work:

Taking the same order in which the signs on the ecliptic are read today when Aries has become *Princeps Zodiaci* we can identify at least a dozen of the deities of Egypt with the twelve signs.

1. The ram-headed Amen with the Constellation Aries
2. Osiris, the Bull of Eternity with Taurus.
3. The Sut-Horus twins with the Gemini.
4. The beetle-headed Kheper-Ptah with the sign of the Beetle, later, Crab.

5. The lion-faced Atum with Leo.
6. The Virgin Neith with the constellation Virgo.
7. Har-Makhu of the Scales with the sign of Libra.
8. Isis-Serkh, the scorpion goddess with the sign of Scorpio
9. Shu and Tefnut, figured as the Archer with the sign of Sagittarius.
10. Num, the goat-headed, who presided over the abyss, with the sign of Capricornus.
11. Menat, the divine wetnurse with the sign Aquarius.
12. Horus, of the two crocodiles, with the sign of Pisces.

(Massey, *Ancient Egypt,* Vol. I, p. 302)

The role of the zodiacal symbolism in ancient mythology and religion was revealed to the modern world by a French scholar, Charles François Dupuis (1742-1809), who wrote a twelve volume work entitled *The Origin of All Religious Worship.* A one-volume abridgment, translated into English, was published in New Orleans in 1872 and extracts from this translation have recently been reprinted in *The Rise of Modern Mythology,* by Burton Feldman and Robert D. Richardson. Count Volney was a disciple of Dupuis and popularized many of his ideas in *The Ruins of Empires* (New York: Peter Eckler, 1890). I will refer to this important work again in this essay. Some of the key ideas have been concisely epitomized by Professor Richardson as follows:

Dupuis . . . traced much of Western Civilization, religion, and myth, to the development of the zodiac. He argued, the zodiac must have arisen in North Africa, in Upper Egypt and Ethiopia, about fifteen-thousand years ago, since the constellations and their signs were matched best at that time and place . . . The zodiac, Dupuis thought, was an astronomical and agricultural calendar, the first most important schematization of the astral, solar and lunar events that interested early man, and the general source of most early stories, personifications, and myths. Early man according to Dupuis, worshipped nature and the forces of nature: he did not worship some abstract or nonexistent force behind or above nature. (Burton

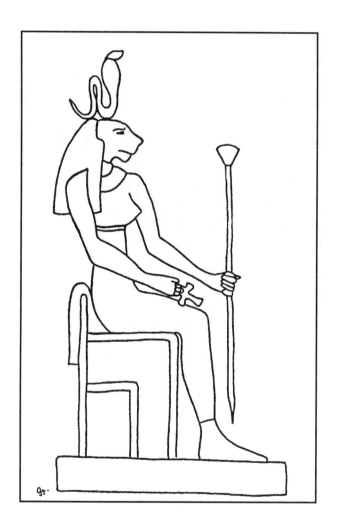

**Tefnut**

**Shu**

Feldman and Robert D. Richardson, *The Rise of Modern Mythology*, Bloomington, Ind.: Indiana University Press, 1972, pp. 276-277.)

The theoretical position taken by Dupuis was brilliantly defended by his disciple, Volney, and at a later date by Massey and Churchward. The classic statement on the origin of the zodiacal system was given by Count Volney in his celebrated *Ruins of Empires*, and since that work is now out of print I reproduce the following eloquent passage:

Should it be asked at what epoch this system took its birth, we shall answer on the testimony of the monuments of astronomy itself, that its principles appear with certainty to have been established about seventeen thousand years ago. And if it be asked to what people it is to be attributed, we shall answer that the same monuments, supported by the unanimous traditions, attribute it to the first tribes of Egypt; and when reason finds in that country all the circumstances which could lead to such a system; when it finds there a zone of sky, bordering on the tropic, equally free from the rains of the equator and the fogs of the North; when it finds there a central point of the sphere of the ancients, a salubrious climate, a great, but manageable river, a soil fertile without art or labor, inundated without morbid exhalations, and placed between two seas which communicate with the richest countries, it conceives that the inhabitant of the Nile, addicted to agriculture from the nature of his soil, to geometry from the annual necessity of measuring his lands, to commerce from the facility of communciations, to astronomy from the state of the sky, always open to observation, must have been the first to pass from the savage to the social state; and consequently to attain the physical and moral sciences necessary to civilized life.

It was, then, on the borders of the Upper Nile, among a black race of men, that was organized the complicated system of the worship of the stars, considered in relation to the productions of the earth and the labors of agriculture; and this first worship, characterized by their adoration under their own forms and natural attributes, was a simple proceeding of the human mind....

As soon as this agricultural people began to observe the stars with attention, they found it necessary to individualize or group them; and to assign to each a proper name. . . A great difficulty must have presented itself . . . First, the heavenly bodies, similar in form, offered no distinguishing characteristics by which to denominate them; and secondly, the language in its infancy and poverty had no expressions for so many new and metaphysical ideas. Necessity, the usual stimulus of genius, surmounted everything. Having remarked that in the annual revolution, the renewal and periodic appearance of terrestrial productions were constantly associated with the rising and setting of certain stars, and to their position as relative to the sun, the mind by a natural operation connected in thought these terrestrial and celestial objects, which were connected in fact; and applying to them a common sign, it gave to the stars, and their groups the names of the terrestrial objects by which they answered.

Thus the Ethiopian of Thebes named stars of inundation, or Aquarius, those stars under which the Nile began to overflow; stars of the ox or bull, those under which they began to plow; stars of the lion, those under which that animal, driven from the desert by thirst, appeared on the banks of the Nile; stars of the sheaf, or of the harvest virgin, those of the reaping season; stars of the lamb, stars of the two kids, those under which these precious animals were brought forth....

Thus the same Ethiopian having observed that the return of the inundation always corresponded with the rising of a beautiful star which appeared towards the source of the Nile, and seemed to warn the husbandman against the coming waters, he compared this action to that of the animal which, by his barking, gives notice of danger, and he called this star the dog, the barker (Sirius). In the same manner he named the stars of the crab, those where the sun, having arrived at the tropic, retreated by a slow retrograde motion like the crab (Cancer). He named stars of the wild goat (Capricorn), those where the sun, having reached the highest point in his annuary tract. . . imitates the goat, which delights to climb to the summit of the rocks. He named stars of the balance (Libra), those were the days and nights, seen being equal, in equilibrium, like that instrument; and stars (Scorpion), those where certain periodical winds bring vapors, burning like the venom of the scorpion. In the same manner he called by the names of rings and serpents the figured traces of the orbits of the stars and planets, and such was the general mode of naming all the stars and even the planets, taken by groups or as individuals, according to their relations with husbandry and terrestrial objects, and according to the analogies which each nation found between them and the objects of its particular soil and climate. (Volney, *The Ruins of Empires,* pp. 120-123.)

The symbolism of the zodiac has been brilliantly displayed in the myth of Hercules, and this myth was known among other peoples: to the Sumerians, Phoenicians, and Greeks. Herodotus named Hercules as being originally one of the great gods of Egypt. There is no god named Hercules in the official pantheon of Egypt, but an ancient Greek tradition identified Hercules with Khonsu, an ancient god of Ethiopian derivation. This deity was a member of the ancient Trinity of Ethiopia: (1) Amen, (2) Nut, and (3) Khonsu. According to St. Clair:

> They were the divinities of Thebes, and that city was hundreds of miles south of Heliopolis; they were the Trinity of Ethiopia and not of Egypt." (George St. Clair, *Creation Records,* p. 404.)

The Hercules saga is best known in its Greek form, but it had more ancient roots in Asia and Africa. Dupuis realized that fact and discussed it with great insight:

> Whatever may have been the opinions about Hercules, he was surely not a petty Grecian prince, renowned for his romantic adventures, invested with all the charms of poetry, and sung from age to age by men, who had succeeded the heroic ages. It is the mighty luminary, which animates and fructifies the Universe, the Divinity of which has been honored

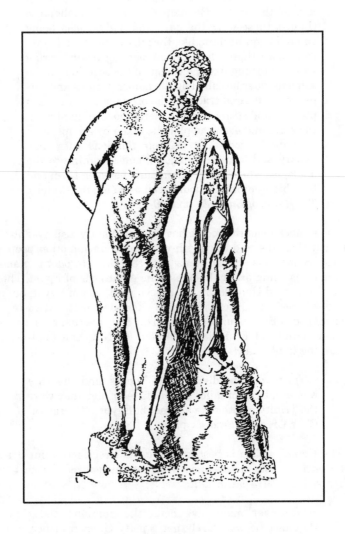

**Hercules**

everywhere by the erection of temples and altars, and consecrated in religious songs in all nations. From Meroë in Ethiopia, and Thebes in Upper Egypt, to the British Isles and to the snows of Scythia; from ancient Taprobane and Palibothra in the Indies to Cadiz and the shores of the Atlantic Ocean; from the forests of Germany to the burning sands of Libya, wherever the blessings of the Sun were experienced, there the worship of Hercules is found established; there are sung the glorious deeds of this invincible God. . . . Many centuries before the epoch, which is assigned to the son of Alcmena or to the supposed hero of Tirynthia, as the time, when they made him live, Egypt and Phoenicia, which surely did not borrow their Gods from Greece, had erected temples to the Sun, under the name of Hercules, and had carried its worship to the island of Thasus and to Cadiz, where they had also consecrated a temple to the Year and to the Month, which divided it into twelve parts, or in other words, to the twelve labors, or twelve victories, which conducted Hercules to immortality . . . The titles of the King of Fire, of Lord of the World, and of the Planets — of nourisher of mankind, of the God, whose glowing orb, revolves eternally about the Earth, and who while followed in his track by the Year, the daughter of Time and Mother of the twelve Months, draws along in regular succession the seasons, which renew and reproduce themselves — are so many traits of the Sun, that we should recognize them, even if the poet had not given to his Hercules the name of Helios or the Sun. (Charles F Dupuis, *The Origin of All Religious Worship,* Abridged Edition, Chapter IV.)

Dupuis was of the opinion that the twelve labors of Hercules were astronomical allegories, myths of the passage of the sun through the twelve signs of the zodiac, and that the story of Jesus Christ in the Bible was equally mythological, since both Jesus and Hercules were sun-gods, and that neither were historical characters. This theory of the non-historicity of Jesus Christ has been ably defended by Count Volney, Lord Bolingbroke, Reverend Robert Taylor, Gerald Massey, Dr. Albert Churchward, Dr. Alvin Boyd Kuhn, John M. Robertson, G . R. S. Mead and several other scholars, equally eminent.

In the myth of Hercules the sun (of which Hercules was the personification) began his zodiacal trip in the constellation Leo, so the first labor of Hercules was the slaying of the Nemean lion. After killing the lion, the hero flayed the beast and used its skin thereafter as a shield. The leonine skin may be compared to the tawny clouds trailed by the sun in fighting his way through atmospheric vapors, which are eventually conquered.

When the sun entered Virgo, the constellation of Hydra was setting, and, thus, the second labor of Hercules was to kill the Lernean Hydra. The monster had several heads, one being immortal, and as he raised them to attack Hercules, the hero burned off the mortal heads and buried the immortal one under a stone. The esoteric meaning of this has been explained by Olcott as follows:

> As the beast was possessed by many heads, so the storm wind must continually supply new clouds to vanquish the sun, but the lighter vapor and mist, the immortal head, is only conquered for a time. The sun easily burns up the heavy clouds, the mortal heads, but only hides temporarily the immortal head, which rises again and again to daunt him. In the fight Hercules was attended by his friend Iolus; this name recalls Iole, signifying the violet tinted clouds, the attendants of the sun in its serene moments. (William Tyler Olcott, *Sunlore of All Ages,* New York: G. P. Putnam Sons, 1914, pp. 72-73.)

The sun entered Libra at the commencement of Autumn at the time when the constellation of the Centaur rose above the horizon, so, Hercules in his third labor was entertained by a centaur and soon afterwards he slew a group of centaurs in a fight over a cask of wine. When the sun was in Libra a star-group called the Boar appeared in the evening sky, so, after killing the centaurs, Hercules met the Erymanthian boar and engaged him in mortal combat.

As the sun moved into Scorpio, Cassiopeia, more anciently known as the Stag, rose into view, and the fourth labor of Hercules was the capture of a stag with golden horns and brazen feet.

As the sun passed into Sagittarius, three constellations named after birds followed, and these were the Vulture, the Swan and the Eagle. In his fifth labor Hercules killed three birds with arrows.

The constellation Capricorn was also called the Stable of Augeas, and the sixth labor of Hercules was the cleaning out of the Augean Stable.

While the sun was in Aquarius, the Lyre, or celestial Vulture, proceeded to set. Prometheus at the time was also setting, while the Bull of Europa was on the meridian. In his seventh labor Hercules slew the vulture which had preyed on the liver of Prometheus and captured a wild bull engaged in laying waste the island of Crete.

While the sun was going through Pisces, Pegasus, the celestial horse, rose in the east, so in the eighth labor Hercules absconded with the horses of Diomede.

As the sun entered Aries (the Ram of the Golden Fleece), the Ship Argo was rising in the evening sky and Andromeda was setting. One of the stars in Andromeda was called her girdle. In his ninth labor Hercules sailed in the Ship Argo in search of the Golden Fleece; he also fought the Amazons and captured the girdle of Hippolyte, their queen, and then rescued Hesione from a sea monster, just as Perseus did Andromeda.

As the sun passed into the Bull, the Pleiades rose and Orion set, and the tenth Herculean labor was to restore the seven kidnapped Pleiades to their father after killing their abductor, King Busiris (Orion). Then the burly hero traveled to Spain and appropriated the oxen of Geryon.

When the sun entered Gemini, Sirius (the Dog Star) was rising, and in the eleventh labor Hercules overcame Cerberus, the guardian dog of Hades.

As the sun entered into the constellation Cancer, the River and the Centaur were setting in the western sky. The constellation Hercules also descended toward the west, followed by Draco (the Dragon of the North Pole) and guardian of the Golden Apples of the Hesperides. In star atlases Hercules had been pictured as crushing the head of a dragon with one of his feet. In the twelfth and final labor Hercules journeys to the Hesperides in quest of the Golden Apples of that region. Afterwards he donned a robe, which was soaked in the blood of a centaur slain by him at the river crossing. The robe mysteriously caught fire, and Hercules perished in the flames. This death ended his mortal career, but later on he resumed his youth in Heaven, and there became immortal. The death scene of this solar deity has been compared to the description of a beautiful sunset, by an outstanding authority on astronomical mythology:

> In this death scene of the solar hero, and in the glories of his funeral pyre, we have the most famous sunset scene that has ever been presented for our contemplation. All the wondrous coloring that adorns the western sky at set of sun illuminated the canvas, and the reflection of the scene streams afar, lighting the

waves of the Aegean and its clustering Isles, and painting in enduring hues a scene that all nations proclaim the sublimest that nature offers, to man's vision. (William Tyler Olcott, *Sunlore of All Ages*, p. 74.)

The myth of the Hindu sun-god Krishna has also been interpreted as an allegory of the annual passage of the sun through the twelve signs of the Zodiac. The classic statement of this thesis was made by Count Volney, whom I cite at length:

> By these records, the first authors had understood the annual revolution of the great celestial orb called the world (a revolution composed of twelve months or signs, divided each into a thousand parts), and the two systematic periods, of winter and summer, composed each of six thousand. These expressions, wholly equivocal and badly explained, having received an absolute and moral, instead of a physical and astrological sense, it happened that the annual world was taken for the secular world, the thousand of the zodiacal divisions, for a thousand of years; and supposing, from the state of things, that they lived in the age of evil, they inferred that it would end with the six thousand pretended years.

> Now, according to calculations admitted by the Jews, they began to reckon near six thousand years since the supposed creation of the world. This coincidence caused a fermentation in the public mind. Nothing was thought of but the approaching end. They consulted the hierophants and the mystical books, which differed as to the term; the great mediator, the final judge, was expected and desired, to put an end to so many calamities. This being was so much spoken of, that some person finally was said to have seen him; and a first rumor of this sort was sufficient to establish a general certainty. Popular report became an established fact; the imaginary being was realized; and all the circumstances of mythological tradition, being assembled around this phantom, produced a regular history, of which it was no longer permitted to doubt.

These mythological traditions recounted that, in the beginning, a woman and a man had by their fall introduced sin and misery into the world. By this was denoted the astronomical fact, that the celestial Virgin (Virgo) and the Herdsman (Bootes), by setting heliacally at the autumnal equinox, delivered the world to the wintry constellations, and seemed, on falling below the horizon, to introduce into the world the genius of evil, Ahrimanes, represented by the constellation of the Serpent.

These traditions related that the woman had decoyed and seduced the man. And in fact, the Virgin, setting first, seems to draw the Herdsman after her. They said that the woman tempted him by offering him fruit fair to the sight and good to eat, which gave the knowledge of good and evil.

And in fact, the Virgin holds in her hand a branch of fruit, which she seems to offer to the Herdsman; and the branch, emblem of autumn . . . seems to open the door and give knowledge, the key of good and evil.

It was said that this couple had been driven from the celestial garden, and that a cherub with a flaming sword had been placed at the gate to guard it. And in fact, when the Virgin and the Herdsman fall beneath the horizon, Perseus rises on the other side; and this Genius, with a sword in his hand, seems to drive them from the summer heaven, the garden and dominion of fruits and flowers.

Of this Virgin should be born, spring up, an off-spring, a child, who should bruise the head of the serpent, and deliver the world from sin. This denotes the sun, which at the moment of the Winter Solstice, precisely when the Persian Magi drew the horoscope of the New Year, was placed on the bosom of the Virgin, rising heliacally on the eastern horizon; on this account he was figured in their astrological picture under the form of a child suckled by a chaste virgin, and became afterwards, at the Vernal Equinox, the Ram, or the Lamb, triumphant over the constellation of the Serpent, which disappeared from the skies.

In his infancy, this restorer of divine and celestial nature would live abased, humble, obscure and indigent. And this, because the winter sun is abased below the horizon; and that this first period of his four ages or seasons, is time of obscurity, scarcity, fasting, and want. That, being put to death by the wicked he had risen gloriously; that he had reascended from hell to heaven, where he would reign forever. This is a sketch of the life of the Sun; who, finishing his career at the Winter Solstice, when Typhon and the rebel angels gain the dominion, seems to be put to death by them; but who soon after is reborn again, and rises into the vault of heaven, where he reigns.

Finally, these traditions went so far as to mention even his astrological and mythological names, and inform us that he was called sometimes Chris, that is to say, preserver, and from that, ye Indians, you have made your god Chris-en or Crish-na; and ye Greek and Western Christians, your Christos, son of Mary, is the same; sometimes he is called *Yes,* by the union of three letters, which by their numerical value form the number 608, one of the solar periods. And this, Europeans, is the name which, with the Latin termination, is become your Yes-us or Jesus, the ancient and cabalistic name attributed to young Bacchus, the clandestine son (nocturnal) of the Virgin Minerva, who, in the history of his whole life, and even of his death, brings to mind the history of the god of the Christians, that is, of the star of day, of which they are each of them the emblems. (Volney, *The Ruins of Empires,* pp. 155-160.)

Following the passage cited above, Count Volney in a footnote made reference to an "Ode to the Sun" by the Roman poet Martianus Capella. Fortunately, there is a good English translation of this tribute to the solar orb, which I reproduce below from an authoritative source:

Latium invokes thee, *Sol,* because thou alone art in honor, *after the Father,* the centre of light; and they affirm that thy sacred head bears a golden brightness in twelve rays, because thou formest that number of months and that number of hours. They say that thou guidest four winged steeds, because thou alone rulest the chariot of the elements. For, dispelling the darkness, thou revealest the shining heavens. Hence they esteem thee, Phoebus, the discoverer of the secrets of the future; or, because thou preventest nocturnal crimes. Egypt worships thee as Serapis, and Memphis as Osiris. Thou art worshipped by different rites as Mithra, Dis, and the cruel Typhon. Thou art alone the beautiful Atys, and the fostering son of the bent plough. Thou art the Ammon of arid Libya, and the Adonis of Byblus. *Thus under a varied appellation the whole world worships thee.* Hail! thou true image of the gods, and of thy father's face! Thou whose sacred name, surname, and omen, three letters make to agree with the number 608. Grant us, oh Father, to reach the eternal intercourse of mind, and to know the starry heaven under this sacred name. May the great and universally adorable Father increase these his favors. (T. W Doane, *Bible Myths,* p. 507.)

In a footnote, on the same page, Doane stated that:

These three letters, the monogram of the Sun, are the celebrated I.H.S., which are to be seen in Roman Catholic churches at the present day, and which are now the monogram of the Sun-god *Christ* Jesus.

The church authorities translated these symbols as *Jesus Hominem Salvator* (Jesus the Savior of Men). The ancient students of esoteric religion read them as the number 608; the time period of a solar-lunar cycle; the number of years which pass before the sun and moon occupy the same relative position in the heavens. The cycle 608 (or 600) years represented a messianic period, at the end of which a new savior or messiah appeared on earth. The letters IHS were the sacred monogram of the Greek god Bacchus. The Christians adopted them and made them the root of the name Jesus. The IHS when Latinized became IES, and adding the Latin masculine suffix -US, that is IES plus US, became IESUS. When anglicized, the "I" became "J" thus giving JESUS.

Count Volney seems to have thought that the story of Jesus Christ, as related in the New Testament, was directly derived from the biography of Krishna as recorded in the sacred books of ancient India. Volney's argument seems to have been based on a false etymology of the resemblance between the words Krishna and Christ. The late John M. Robertson wrote a learned treatise entitled *Christ and Krishna,* and in that work he argued that there was no direct contact between Krishnaism and Christianity; but that both cults were derived from an earlier common source. Robertson suggested ancient Egypt as the possible earliest home of these Savior-God religions.

Gerald Massey and his school have argued persuasively for an Egyptian origin of Christianity, claiming that the whole Christian Bible, both Old and New Testaments, are traceable to the religious records of ancient Egypt. Massey presented his opinions backed up by impressive documentation. I cannot discuss these works at length, for that would require a book in itself. However, Massey did publish a book of ten lectures; the most important being *The Historical Jesus and the Mythical Christ.* I shall discuss this work briefly because of its importance in the study of the myth theory of Christian origins. Massey noted that two birthdays had been assigned to Jesus by the Christian Fathers; one at the Winter Solstice (Christmas), and the other at the Vernal Equinox (Easter); and he observed:

> These, which cannot both be historical, are based on the two birthdays of the double Horus in Egypt. Plutarch tells us that Isis was delivered of Horus the child, about the time of the Winter Solstice, and that the festival of the second or adult Horus followed the Vernal Equinox. Hence the Solstice and Spring Equinox were both assigned to the one birth of Jesus by the Christolators; and again, that which is impossible as human history is the natural fact in relation to the two Horuses, the dual form of the Solar God in Egypt. (Massey, *Lectures,* p. 6.)

The relation between Osiris, Horus and Jesus, along with the astronomical elements underlying the mythology, is explained thusly:

> In Egypt the year began just after the Summer Solstice, when the sun descended from its midsummer height, lost its force, and lessened in its size. This represented Osiris, who was born of the Virgin Mother as the child Horus, the diminished infantile sun of Autumn; the suffering, wounded, bleeding Messiah, as he was represented. He descended into

hell, or hades, where he was transformed into the virile Horus, and rose again as the sun of the resurrection at Easter. In these two characters of Horus on the two horizons, Osiris furnished the dual type for the Canonical Christ, which shows very satisfactorily how the mythical prescribes the boundaries beyond which the historical does not, dare not, go. The first was the child Horus, who always remained a child. In Egypt the boy or girl wore the Horus lock of childhood until twelve years of age. Thus childhood ended about the twelfth year. But although adultship was then entered upon by the youth, and the transformation of the boy into manhood began, the full adultship was not attained until thirty years of age. The man of thirty years was the typical adult. As with the man, so it is with the God; and the second Horus, the same God in his second character, is the *Khemt* or *Khem-Horus,* the typical adult of thirty years. The God up to twelve years was Horus, the child of Isis, the mother's child, the weakling. The virile Horus (the sun in its vernal strength), the adult of thirty years, was representative of the Fatherhood, and this Horus is the anointed son of Osiris. These two characters of Horus the child, and Horus the adult of thirty years, are reproduced in the only two phases of the life of Jesus in the Gospels . . . and these two characters of Horus necessitated a double form of the mother, who divides into the two divine sisters, Isis and Nephthys. Jesus also was - bimater; or dual-mothered; and the two sisters reappear in the Gospels, as the two Maries, both of whom are the mothers of Jesus. This again, which is impossible as human history, is perfect according to the mythos that explains it.

As the child Horus, Osiris comes down to earth; he enters matter and becomes mortal. He is born like the Logos or as a Word. His father is Seb, the earth, whose consort is Nut, the heaven, one of whose names is Meri, the Lady of Heaven; and these two are the prototypes of Joseph and Mary. He is said to cross the earth a substitute, and to suffer vicariously as the Savior, Redeemer, and Justifier of men. In these two characters there was constant conflict between Osiris and Sut, the Egyptian Satan. At the Autumnal

Equinox the devil of darkness began to dominate; this was the Egyptian Judas, who betrayed Osiris to his death at the last supper. On the day of the Great Battle at the Vernal Equinox, Osiris conquered as the ascending God, the Lord of the growing light. Both these struggles are portrayed in the Gospels. In the one Jesus is betrayed to his death by Judas; in the other he rises superior to Satan. The latter conflict followed immediately after the baptism. In this way: when the sun was half way round from the Lion sign, it crossed the River of the Waterman, the Egyptian Iarutana, Hebrew Jordan, Greek Eridanus. In this water the baptism occurred, and the transformation of the child — Horus into the virile adult; the conqueror of the evil power, took place, Horus became hawk-headed, just where the dove ascended and abode on Jesus; both birds represented the virile soul that constituted the anointed one at puberty. By this added power Horus vanquished Sut and Jesus overcame Satan. (Massey, *Lectures*, pp. 13-15.)

Since the mythology of Horus was known in Egypt thousands of years before the advent of Christianity, then the Egyptian Christ must have been the original and the Christian Christ a copy of the much earlier prototype. This viewpoint again was cogently presented by Massey in the following passage:

The Christian dispensation is believed to have been ushered in by the birth of a child, and the portrait of that child in the Roman catacombs as the child of Mary is the youthful Sun-God in the Mummy image of the child-king, the Egyptian Karast, or Christ. The alleged facts of our Lord's life as Jesus the Christ, were equally the alleged facts of our Lord's life as the Horus of Egypt, whose very name signifies the Lord. . . Whether you believe or not does not matter, the fatal fact remains that every trait and feature which go to make up the Christ as Divinity, and every event or circumstance taken to establish the human personality were pre-extant and pre-applied to the Egyptian and Gnostic Christ, who never could become flesh. The Jesus Christ with female paps, who is the Alpha and Omega of Revelation, was the *Iu* of Egypt and the *Iao* of the Chaldeans. Jesus as the Lamb of God, and Ichthys the

Fish, was Egyptian. Jesus as the Coming One; Jesus born of the Virgin Mother, who was overshadowed by the Holy Ghost; Jesus born of two mothers, both of whose names are Mary; Jesus born in the manger, at Christmas and again at Easter; Jesus saluted by the three kings, or Magi; Jesus of the transfiguration on the Mount; Jesus whose symbol in the Catacombs is the eight-rayed star — the Star of the East; Jesus as the eternal child; Jesus as God the Father, reborn as his own Son; Jesus as the Child of twelve years; Jesus as the Anointed One of thirty years; Jesus in his Baptism; Jesus walking on the waters, or working his Miracles; Jesus as the Caster-out of demons; Jesus as a Substitute, who suffered in a vicarious atonement for sinful men; Jesus whose followers are the two brethren, the four fishers, the seven fishers, the twelve apostles, the seventy (or seventy-two in some texts) whose names were written in Heaven; Jesus who was administered to by seven women; Jesus in his bloody sweat; Jesus betrayed by Judas; Jesus as conqueror of the grave; Jesus the Resurrection and the Life; Jesus before Herod; in Hades, and in his reappearance to the women, and to the seven fishers; Jesus who was crucified both on the 14th and 15th of the month Nisan; Jesus who was also crucified in Egypt (as it is written in Revelation); Jesus as judge of the dead, with the sheep on the right hand, and the goats on the left, is Egyptian from first to last, in every phase, from the beginning to the end. (Massey, *Lectures,* pp. 21-22.)

The worship of Osiris and Isis was popular in the Roman Empire for hundreds of years, and the Greeks got many of their gods from the Egyptians, but neither the Romans nor the Greeks really understood the symbolism or mythology of the Egyptians. These Europeans turned the gods into men, and the esoteric meaning of the old religion was lost; hence the ancient beliefs finally passed into a state of innocuous desuetude. The old gods after being humanized became objects of ridicule rather than adoration. Some remarks of Sir Wallis Budge on the decline of ancient Egyptian faith may appropriately be cited here:

> There must have been large numbers of people who scoffed at the animal forms of the Egyptian gods, and at the extraordinary symbols and ceremonies which

appertained to their cult. The feelings of such are voiced by Lucian in his short work, *The Council of the Gods,* in which he described a meeting of the three gods, Zeus, Hermes and Momus, to discuss the complaints made by the last named to the effect that the banquet of the gods had been thrown open to a number of undesirable persons. Momus, the Accuser General, complained that many persons, in spite of their mixed origin, had been admitted to the feasts and councils of the gods upon terms of equality, that such had brought with them their servants and satellites and enrolled them among the gods; and that these menials shared in their rations and sacrifices without even so much as paying the customary tax. Momus went so far as to point out to Zeus that the mixed state of society among the gods was due to him and his terrestrial gallantries, and that heaven was simply swarming with the demi-gods whom Zeus had introduced. It was all the result of the attentions paid by him to the daughters of Earth, and the goddesses were just as bad as the gods. Momus then went on to comment unfavorably on Dionysus, Attis, Corybus, Sabazius and Mithra and then went on to attack the gods of Egypt. He said: 'I shall just like to ask that Egyptian there — the dog faced gentleman in the linen suit (Anubis) who he is, and whether he proposes to establish his divinity by barking? And will the piebald bull yonder (Apis), from Memphis, explain what *he* has for a temple, an oracle, or a priest? As for the ibises, and monkeys and goats, and worse absurdities that are bundled upon us, goodness knows how, from Egypt, I am ashamed to speak of them; nor do I understand how you, gentlemen, can endure to see such creatures enjoying a prestige equal to or greater than your own. And you yourself, sir, must surely find ram's horns a great inconvenience?" To this Zeus replied that the way in which the Egyptians went on was disgraceful, but he reminded Momus that there was an occult significance in most of these things, and that it ill became him, who was not one of the initiates, to ridicule them. To this Momus tartly replied: "A god is one thing, and a person with a dog's head is another; I need no initiation to tell me that."

In spite, however, of all gibes and jeers, and ridicule, the cult of Osiris and Isis spread all over Southern

Europe, and into many parts of North Africa, and it continued to be a religious power in them until the close of the fourth century A.D. At Philae . . . the worship of Osiris and Isis continued until the reign of Justinian, and it only came to an end in Nubia then, because the Emperor caused the temple to be closed by force, and confiscated the revenues of the shrine. The ideas and beliefs which were the foundations of the cult were not even then destroyed, for they survived in Christianity. And the bulk of the masses in Egypt and Nubia who professed Christianity transferred to Mary the Virgin, the attributes of Isis the Everlasting Mother, and to the Babe Jesus, those of Horus. About the middle of the Ptolemaic Period the attributes of Osiris were changed, and after his identification with Seraphis, *i.e.,* Pluto, the god of death, his power and influence declined rapidly, for he was no longer the god of life. In the final state of the cult of Osiris and Isis, the former was the symbol of Death and the latter the symbol of Life. (E. A. Wallis Budge, Osiris: *The Egyptian Religion of The Resurrection,* New York: University Books, 1961, Vol. II, pp. 305–306.)

The literature on the Osirian cult is rather large. For the novice the best introductions would be James George Frazer, *Adonis, Attis, Osiris,* (New Hyde Park, NY: University Books, 1961), and Harold P. Cooke, *Osiris: A Study in Myths, Mysteries and Religion,* (London: The C. W. Daniel Co., 1931).

**Zeus**

# Chapter XII
## Comments and Conclusion

In 1921 when Dr. Albert Churchward in his *The Origin and Evolution of the Human Race,* announced that Africa was the cradle of the human species and that mankind had emerged from the apes in the so-called Dark continent at least two million years ago, he was shouted down by his anthropological colleagues. Churchward also stated that the first true men were the Pygmies of Africa. This was also denied by the recognized experts. But it has turned out that Dr. Churchward was correct on both counts. The researches and discoveries of Dr. Raymond Dart, Dr. Robert Broom, Professor Louis Leakey, Mrs. Mary Leakey, Richard Leakey, and others has established the high probability that mankind emerged in Africa between four and five million years ago. The African origin of man had been predicted in 1871 by Charles Darwin in *The Descent of Man.* This opinion was augmented by Gerald Massey in 1883:

> Africa, and not Asia, was the birthplace of articulate man, and therefore the primordial home of all things human, and the race that ranged out over the world, including the islands of the North and the lands of the Southern Seas was directly Kamite; the Blacks of Britain (who left flattened tibia, the Negroid pelvis, the Australoid molars and gorilla-like molars in the bone caves), and the Blacks of Australia, being two extreme wings extended from the same African center. Professor Huxley recognized in the native Egyptian the most refined form of the same anthropological type that survives at a far lower stage in the Australian Black. My further contention is that both issue from inner Africa as the human birthplace. (Massey, *The Natural Genesis,* Vol. I, pp. 8-9.)

Dr. Albert Churchward, for many years a research associate of Gerald Massey, concluded after much study that:

> The first or Paleolithic man was the pygmy, who was evolved in Central Africa at the sources of the Nile, or Nile Valley, and that from here all originated, and were carried throughout the world. (Churchward, *The Signs and Symbols of Primordial Man,* p. 3.)

Churchward also claimed that the earliest religion could be traced to the same source:

> Now we cannot get back further in the origin of reli-
> gion, its meanings and true interpretation than the
> Pygmies, for the Pygmy was the first human in evo-
> lution from the Anthropoid Ape. Here then we find
> the origin and dawn of all religion and religious ideas
> . . . These Pygmies are upon the lowest step in the
> ascent of man. They were the first humans, and
> although still found in many parts of the world, their
> Motherland is Africa. In no other country do we find
> even any trace of the connecting links (Bushman and
> Masaba Negro) with the Nilotic Negro who developed
> religious ideas in the next stage of evolution. So closely
> were the facts of nature observed and registered by
> the Egyptians that the earliest divine men in their
> mythology are portrayed as Pygmies, and the earliest
> form of the Human Mother was depicted with the
> characteristics of the Pygmy woman. (Dr. Albert
> Churchward, *The Origin and Evolution of Religion*,
> London: George Allen & Unwin, 1924, pp. 7-8.)

The anthropologist Jean-Pierre Hallet lived among the Pygmies of the Ituri Forest of the Congo region for twenty years. We judge from what he learned that the original form of Christianity origi-nated among these people:

> My Pygmy friends have an Adam story of their own
> . . . It is the story of a god, a garden paradise, a sacred
> tree, a noble Pygmy man, who was molded from the
> dust of the earth, and a wicked Pygmy woman who
> led him into sin . . . The legend tells of the ban placed
> by God upon a single fruit, the woman's urging, the
> man's reluctance, the original sin, the discovery by
> God, and the awful punishment he laid upon the anci-
> ent Pygmy sinners; the loss of immortality and para-
> dise, the pangs of childbirth, and the curse of hard
> work. (Jean-Pierre Hallet, *Pygmy Kitabu*, Greenwich,
> Connecticut: Fawcett Publications, 1975, p. 37.)

The Pygmies believed in a Father-God who was murdered, and a Virgin Mother, who gave birth to a Savior-God Son, who in turn avenged the death of his father. These later on became the Osiris, Isis and Horus of Egypt. The Pygmy Christ was born of a virgin, died for the salvation of his people, arose from the dead, and finally ascended to heaven. Certainly this looks like Christianity before Christ.

Hallet's Pygmy friends told him that in the distant past they developed a highly technical and advanced type of material culture and that they built boats and traveled widely over the world, but that this technical excellence brought them nothing but bad luck, so, preferring happiness to misery, they finally gave up this high material civilization. There may be a lot of truth in these traditions, for Pygmy fossils have been found in all parts of the world. How did these so-called primitive people spread over the world if they had no boats? Certainly they did not swim across the various oceans. These ancient little men were certainly not savages. In the words of Georg:

> A splendid era of Blacks seems to have preceded all the later races. There must once have been a tremendous Negro expansion, since the original masters of the lands between Iberia and the Cape of Good Hope and East India were primitive and probably dwarfed Black men. We have long had proof that a primitive Negroid race of Pygmies once lived around the Mediterranean. Blacks were the first to plow the mud of the Nile; they were the dark-skinned, curly-haired Kushites. Blacks were masters of Sumeria and Babylon before it became the country of the four tongues. And in India, the kingdom of the Dravidian monarchs, the Black and godless enemies, existed until the period of written history. (Eugen Georg, *The Adventure of Mankind,* New York: E. P Dutton and Co., 1931, p. 44.)

The ancient Olmec culture of Mexico, obviously of African origin, seemed to have been established by Pygmies. In referring to discoveries made near San Lorenzo and La Venta, A. Hyatt Verrill declared that:

> Most noteworthy of all is a gigantic stone head nine feet in height with eyes two feet in length, and a mouth three feet across and weighing many tons, yet analysis of the rock from which it was carved proves that it was transported overland from the mountains

more than sixty miles away in a beeline. Like all of the stone and pottery heads found in this area the great stone head has thick lips and a broad flat nose of Negroid type, totally unlike the features of any known American race past or present. And like the other stone heads it wears a tightly-fitting cap or helmet similar to the helmets worn by our football players. Another remarkable piece of sculpture from this area was a heroic size figure with a huge serpent on its lap, while the prize of all was a ten ton human figure supposedly representing a deity or priest of the long vanished, forgotten race. As in all the representations of human beings the imposing central figure with its ornate headdress has the typical flat nose and thickened lips ... Among many ancient races, both in the New World and the Old World, dwarfs or pygmies were regarded with more or less superstitious reverence ... According to the present day Mayas of northern Yucatan, they have a tradition that the world was first inhabited by dwarfs ... who, the Mayas believe, built the great cities now in ruins ... Even more interesting is the fact that dwarfs, or abnormally small persons, are quite common among the living Indians of Tabasco. These miniature Indians are about four feet to four and a half feet in height with rather dark skins, broad flat noses and rather thick lips, very similar to those shown in the La Venta sculptures. One of these, a woman whom I knew, was the living replica of a La Venta stone head, and her children — all dwarfs — were very similar. In their actions and behavior they are very much like the Bushmen or Hottentots of Africa, and are inordinately fond of jokes, playing tricks and conversing in pantomime ... Whatever the truth may be, there is no question that the most ancient of the Mexican higher cultures was that of the fat-faced, thick-lipped, flat-nosed people of the La Venta area in the State of Tabasco (A. Hyatt Verrill and Ruth Verrill, *America's Ancient Civilizations*, New York: Capricorn Books, 1967, pp. 97-100.)

The later cultures of the Ethiopians in Africa and Asia seem to have evolved from this more ancient Pygmy culture. There were two Ethiopias in ancient times. To cite Sir Wallis Budge:

It seems certain that classical historians and geographers called the whole region from India to Egypt, both countries inclusive, by the name of Ethiopia, and in consequence they regarded all the dark-skinned and black peoples who inhabited it as Ethiopians. Mention is made of Eastern and Western Ethiopians, and it is probable that the Easterners were Asiatics, and the Westerners, Africans. (E. A. Wallis Budge, *A History of Ethiopia,* London: Methuen and Co., 1928, Vol. I, p. vii.)

Authorities have disagreed on which of the two Ethiopias was the earliest, but now it seems that Africans must be conceded priority. A good statement of this opinion has been made by Lady Lugard:

When the history of Negroland comes to be written in detail, it may be found that the kingdoms lying towards the eastern end of the Sudan were the home of races who inspired, rather than of races who received, the tradition of civilization associated for us with the name of ancient Egypt. For they cover on either side of the Upper Nile between the latitudes of ten degrees and seventeen degrees, territories in which are found monuments more ancient than the oldest Egyptian monuments. If this should prove to be the case and the civilized world be forced to recognize in a black people the fount of its original enlightenment, it may happen that we shall have to revise entirely our view of the black races, and regard those who now exist as the decadent representatives of an almost forgotten era, rather than as the embryonic possibility of an era yet to come. (Lady Lugard, *A Tropical Dependency,* London: Frank Cass and Co., 1964, pp. 17-19.)

The classical home of the ancient Ethiopians was the Eastern Sudan, although Homer and Herodotus mentioned other Ethiopians dwelling in Egypt, Arabia, Palestine, Western Asia and India. Again, to cite Lady Lugard:

The fame of the ancient Ethiopians was widespread in ancient history. Herodotus describes them as the tallest, most beautiful and long-lived of the human races, and before Herodotus, Homer, in even more flattering language, described them as the most just

177

of men, the favorites of the gods. The annals of all the great early nations of Asia Minor are full of them. The Mosaic records allude to them frequently; but while they are described as the most powerful, the most just, and the most beautiful of the human race, they are constantly spoken of as black, and there seems to be no other conclusion to be drawn than that at that remote period of history, the leading race of the Western World was a black race. (Lady Lugard, *A Tropical Dependency*, p. 221)

The ancient Kushite or Ethiopian culture may be called the Archaic Civilization. The outstanding features of this ancient cultural complex were:

1. Agriculture practiced by way of irrigation.
2. The art of carving and building in stone; such as the production of statues, monuments, pyramids, temples palaces, etc.
3. Metal working, especially in iron and steel.
4. The making of pottery.
5. Mummification.
6. The worship of the Great Mother Goddess.
7. The worship of the heavenly bodies: (a) Stars, (b)Planets, (c) the Moon, and (d) the Sun.
8. The prevalence of the institutions of totemism and exogamy.
9. The practice of mother-right.
10.The institution of divine kingship.

(For a detailed discussion of the Archaic Civilization, the reader should consult Professor W. J. Perry, *The Children of the Sun*, New York: E. P Dutton, 1923.) If Perry's work is not available, see John G. Jackson, *Introduction to African Civilizations* (New Hyde Park, NY: University Books, 1970), pp.60-92, and John G. Jackson, *Man, God and Civilization* (New Hyde Park, NY: University Books, 1972), pp. 188-202.

Since the reader may not be familiar with such terms as *totemism, exogamy, mother-right,* and *divine kingship*, I shall devote some space to a discussion of their meanings.

Of the institutions of primitive society, the most important were totemism and exogamy. Totemism was based on a primitive theory of evolution. Firstly, we must ask: What is a totem? There is a considerable literature on the subject, but the clearest definition of totemism was given by Professor Alfred C. Haddon in an address to the Anthropological Section of the British Association for the Advancement of Science:

> Totemism as Dr. Frazer and I understand it in its fully developed condition implies the division of a people into several totem kins (or, as they are usually termed, totem clans), each of which has one or sometimes more than one totem. The totem is usually a species of animal, sometimes a species of plant, occasionally a natural object or phenomenon, very rarely a manufactured article. Totemism also involves the rules of exogamy, forbidding marriage between the kins. It is essentially connected with the matriarchal stage of culture (Mother-Right). The totems are regarded as kins-folk and protectors of the kinsmen, who respect them and abstain from killing and eating them. There is thus a recognition of mutual rights and obligations between the members of the kin, and their totem is the crest or symbol of the kin. (V. F. Calverton's "The Making of Man" in *An Outline of Anthropology*. New York: Modern Library, 1931.)

Certain scholars have referred to totemism as the worship of animals, but this is not correct; animal worship is called zoolatry. In the words of Frazer:

> A man no more worships his totem and regards it as his god than he worships his father and mother, his brother and sister, and regards them as his god. He certainly respects his totem and treats it with consideration, but the respect and consideration which he pays to it are the same that he pays to his friends and relations; hence when a totem is an edible animal or plant, he commonly, but not always, abstains from killing or eating it, just as he commonly, but not always, abstains from killing and eating his friends and relatives. But to call this decent respect for his equals the worship of a god is entirely to misapprehend and misrepresent the essence of totemism. (Frazer, *Totemism and Exogamy*, Vol. IV, London: Macmillan & Co., 1910, p. 5.)

Totemism is an institution that prevails among peoples of dark complexion, inhabiting the tropical lands, the Southern Hemisphere, and parts of North America. With the doubtful exception of some Mongoloid tribes in Assam, there are no yellow or white peoples who practice totemism.

Exogamy is another ancient institution, closely related to Totemism. In primitive societies men and women recognizing the same totem were regarded as brothers and sisters to each other. So, in order to avoid inbreeding, they were required to marry someone who was not a member of their own social group, and this institution seems to have been based on group marriage. Exogamy meant marriage outside the group, in contradistinction to endogamy, which was marriage inside the group. Exogamy probably arose when a local group whose totem was, say, a bear, intermarried with another local group whose totem, say, was a bull. Each group was a clan; then by intermarriage they formed a tribe. With matrilineal descent, which was the earliest type of kinship, the totems would alternate from one generation to another. The result would be as tabulated:

|  | *The Bull Clan* | *The Bear Clan* |
|---|---|---|
| 1st Generation: | Bull | Bear |
| 2nd Generation: | Bear | Bull |
| 3rd Generation: | Bull | Bear |
| 4th Generation: | Bear | Bull |

To prevent endogamy the tribe would divide into two moieties (halves).

### Tribe

| *Bull Moiety* Generations | *Bear Moiety* Generations |
|---|---|
| 1st and 3rd: Bull | 1st and 3rd: Bear |
| 2nd and 4th: Bear | 2nd and 4th: Bull |

This practice would automatically divide the tribe into four divisions, two in each moiety, as listed below:

### Tribe

| *Moiety: A* Generations | *Moiety: B* Generations |
|---|---|
| 1st and 3rd: Bull | 1st and 3rd: Bear |
| 2nd and 4th: Bear | 2nd and 4th: Bull |

From the above scheme we obtain a breakup of the tribe into four divisions, two in each moiety:

### Tribe

| Moiety: A | Moiety: B |
|---|---|
| DIVISION I<br>1st Generation | DIVISION I<br>1st Generation |
| 3rd Generation | 3rd Generation |
| DIVISION II<br>2nd Generation | DIVISION II<br>2nd Generation |
| 4th Generation | 4th Generation |

The above data gives an idea of the two-class system of exogamy. Four-class and eight-class systems exist in Australia, and nowhere else; they are somewhat complicated and I need not discuss them here.

The practice of tracing kinship and inheritance through women has been called *mother-right*. The opposite custom of tracing kinship and inheritance through men is known as *father-right*. The matriarchal system is much older than the patriarchal, since in ancient times when group marriage was widespread, it was either difficult or impossible to ascertain paternity.

In ancient Ethiopia and Egypt the kings were gods. The divine kingship seems to have originated in Africa and as recently as one hundred years ago it still thrived in Uganda. Among the ancient Ethiopians of Africa the divine kingship survived until the third century B.C. when King Ergamanes brought it to an end. The story of how this came about was recorded by the Greek historian Diodorus Siculus, who, in discussing Ethiopian mores, declared that:

> Of all their customs the most astonishing is that which obtains in connection with the death of their kings. For the priests at Meroë who spend their time in the worship of the gods and the rites which do them honor, being the greatest and most powerful order, whenever the idea comes to them, dispatch a messenger to the king with orders that he die. For the gods, they add, have revealed this to them, and it must be

that the command of the immortals should in no wise be disregarded by one of mortal frame. And this order they accompany with other arguments, such as are accepted by a simple-minded nature, which has been bred in a custom that is both ancient and difficult to eradicate, and which knows no argument that can be set in opposition to commands enforced by no compulsion. Now in former times the kings would obey the priests, having been overcome, not by arms nor by force, but because of their very superstition; but during the reign of the second Ptolemy, the King of the Ethiopians, Ergamenes, who had had a Greek education and had studied philosophy, was the first to have the courage to disdain the command. For assuming a spirit which became the position of a king, he entered with his soldiers into the unapproachable place, where stood, as it turned out, the golden shrine of the Ethiopians, put the priests to the sword, and after abolishing this custom thereafter ordered affairs after his own will. (Diodorus Siculus, *Library of History,* Vol. II, Book III, pp. 101–103.)

According to Diodorus, the Ethiopians were the earliest of civilized men, and that they colonized Egypt under the leadership of Osiris. Then the Egyptians diffused this Ethiopian culture to all parts of the world. There is an interesting commentary on the latter statement by Dr. Churchward:

Diodorus Siculus declares that the Egyptians claimed to have sent out colonies over the whole world in times of the remotest antiquity. They affirmed that they had not only taught the Babylonians astronomy, but that Belus and his subjects were a colony that went out of Egypt. This is also supported by the book of Genesis in the generations of Noah. He was greatly impressed with the assertions of the priests respecting the numerous emigrations, including the colonies of Babylon and Greece, but they named so many in diverse parts of the world that he shrank from recording them upon hearsay and word of mouth. He tells us that they had sacred books transmitted to them from ancient times in which the historical accounts were recorded and kept, and then handed on to their successors. . . .

Thus we see that colonies went forth and settled in all parts of the world, leaving the proofs in language, myth, and the hieroglyphics, in religious rites. The symbolical customs and ceremonies in far off lands are still extant among races by whom they are no longer read or understood, but which can be read in Egypt. *(The Signs and Symbols of Primordial Man,* pp. 283-284)

Herodotus was told by Egyptian scribes that they had astronomical records going back 50,000 years. We cannot check these figures, but certainly the Egyptian astronomers had accurate records, going back to a remote past. Later on, Diodorus observed:

The positions and arrangements of the stars as well as their motions have always been the subject of careful observation among the Egyptians . . . they have preserved to this day the records concerning each of these stars over an incredible number of years, this subject of study, having been zealously preserved among them from ancient times, and they have also observed with the utmost avidity the motions and orbits and stoppings of the planets . . . And according to them the Chaldeans of Babylon, being colonists from Egypt, enjoy the fame which they have for their astrology because they learned that science from the priests of Egypt. *(Library of History,* Book I, pp. 277-279.)

The data preserved in the Great Pyramid of Egypt shows an advanced knowledge of mathematics and astronomy. Orthodox scholars may deny this, but the evidence exists and it cannot be shouted down. As a well-informed English scholar observed:

Our entire solar system with all its planets and moon describes a huge circle around another sun in space, *viz.,* the star Sirius. This movement takes 25,920 years to complete and, during that time, our Sun appears to traverse through various constellations or star clusters. This was already known to the ancient from China to Mexico and from Babylon to Egypt. (George R. Goodman, "The Age of Unreason," an article in *The Freethinker,* Vol. LXXXV, p. 182.)

In the article cited above Mr. Goodman also discussed the relations of the large and small zodiacs. In discussing the large zodiac he noted that:

By arbitrarily dividing that huge circle into twelve sections (or houses) they gave to each of them an appropriate sign and name and called the duration of 2,160 years an age. Twelve of these ages constitute one complete turn of our solar system around Sirius.

Noting that all religious festivals were and are based on the motions of the sun, moon, planets, and the resulting four seasons, Mr. Goodman then declared:

But for a long time it was something of a mystery why practically all Sun-gods and most of the Christs and Messiahs should have been portrayed as having had two mothers. The answer can be found in the small zodiac. For if one draws a straight line from the zodiac's section called Virgo, going through the pivotal center to the opposite section called Pisces, one has traversed six months, which will presently be seen to dramatize not only cosmic happenings, but also man's evolutionary development.

The ancients localized the birth of the natural man in the zodiacal house of Virgo, and that of the evolved man in the opposite house of Pisces . . . Virgo gave man his natural birth by water (all babies are born in a sac of water!) and became known as the Water-Mother. Pisces stood as the symbol of the evolved and intellectual man and was called the Fish-Mother . . . No wonder then that Virgo was poetised as the Water-Mother of the Natural man, and Pisces as the intellectual and ethically-evolved man or the god-to-be. Man's physical body is the high product of a biological evolution that actually started in the ocean water! The virgin mothers are all identified with water as symbol, and their various names, such as Meri, Mary, Myra, Myrrha, Miriam . . . On the other hand, there are the fish avatars of Vishnu (the second god of the Hindu triad), such as the Babylonian Ioannes who, like the Egyptian Horus and the Gospel Jesus, and the Hebrew Jonah (derived from Ioannes) — all came

as the zodiacal Pisces or Ichthys, *fish* in Greek, and
offered themselves as *food for man* while the latter is
immersed in the sea of generation . . . To put it concisely in one sentence — all the various Christs and
saviors were credited with two mothers, because
Virgo was the watermother of the natural man and
Pisces was the fishmother of the spiritually evolved or
highly ethical and intellectual man . . . But the greatest denouement awaits the investigator who makes
use of the Julian calendar in the Roman Catholic calendar of Saints in connection with the large zodiac.
He will find that the death of John the Baptist is fixed
on August 29th. On that day, a specially bright star,
representing the head of the constellation Aquarius,
rises whilst the rest of his body is below the horizon,
at exactly the same time as the sun sets in Leo (the
kingly sign representing Herod). Thus the latter
*beheads* John, because John is associated with
Aquarius, and *the horizon cuts off the head of
Aquarius!* (Goodman, *The Freethinker,* p. 182.)

Before concluding this essay, something should be said about the
question of the historicity of Jesus Christ. Orthodox Christians
recognize him as a god, Unitarians as a man, and Rationalists as a
myth. An English scholar, Herbert Cutner, wrote an important and
informative book: *Jesus: God, Man or Myth?* (New York: The Truth
Seeker Co., 1950). Mr. Cutner, presenting impressive evidence pro
and con, finally decided that Jesus was a myth. This may come as
a shock to some readers as it did to me when I first came across it
in Gerald Massey's lecture on *The Historical Jesus and The
Mythical Christ.* I tried to refute Massey, but failed completely. The
position taken by the great Egyptologist was found to be impreg-
nable. Massey looked for the Gospel Jesus Christ and could not find
him, but he did discover another Jesus who lived in Egypt about the
year 100 B.C. and met his death by crucifixion. The interested student may study this thesis in Massey's *Lectures,* in G. R. S. Mead's
*Did Jesus Live 100 B.C.?,* and also In Dr. Franz Hartman's *The Life
of Jehoshua: The Prophet of Nazareth* (Boston: Occult Publishing
Co., 1889).

Professor Harry Elmer Barnes, historian and sociologist, after extensive study, finally announced:

> As a matter of fact, the evidence for the point of view that Jesus was actually an historic character is so slight that a considerable number of the most distinguished students of New Testament times have declared Jesus to be a mythological personage. . . . Among the more eminent scholars and critics who have contended that Jesus was not an actual historical figure we mention Bruno Bauer, Kalthoff, Drews, Stendel, Felder, Deyë, Jensen, Lublinski, Bolland, Van der Berg, Virolleaud, Couchoud, Massey, Bossi, Niemojewski, Brandes, Robertson, Mead, Whittaker, Carpenter and W. B. Smith (Harry Elmer Barnes, *The Twilight of Christianity,* New York: Vanguard Press, 1929, pp. 390-391).

Robert Keable, a liberal Christian apologist, wrote a book with the title, *The Great Galilean,* purporting to be a life story of the Christian Christ. Mr. Keable must have drawn heavily on his imagination in order to produce this book, for he tells us right at the start that he had no historical documentation. In his own words:

> No man knows sufficient of the early life of Jesus to write a biography of him. For that matter, no one knows enough for the normal *Times* obituary notice of a great man. If regard were had to what we should call, in correct speech, definitely historical facts, scarcely three lines would be filled.

> Moreover, if newspapers had been in existence, and if that obituary notice had had to be written in the year of his death, no editor could have found in the literature of his day so much as his name. Yet few periods of the ancient world were so well documented as the periods of Augustus and Tiberius. But no contemporary writer knew of his existence. Even a generation later, a spurious passage in Josephus, a questionable reference in Suetonius, and the mention of a name that may be his by Tacitus — that is all. His first mention in any surviving document, secular or religious, is twenty years after.

We do not know with anything approaching historical certainty of whom he was born, or when, or
where; how long he lived, or how long he labored; and
the sayings which are indubitably his are a mere
handful. The stories of his reputed resurrection are so
contradictory and confused that it is impossible to
make more than a guess at their true import. If the
question of his ever having lived at all is not very seri-
ously open to doubt, at least it has been possible for a
Swedish professor within the last few months to
make out a perfectly good case for the supposition
that he was born a century or so before the accepted
date. (Robert Keable, *The Great Galilean* (Boston,
Massachusetts: Little, Brown and Co., 1929, p. 3.)

Orthodox Christians hold that the four Gospels of the New Testament were written by the four evangelists: Matthew, Mark, Luke,
and John. But this cannot be so, for these four characters were not
men. They were, in fact, the four corner signs of the zodiac. The evidence has been presented by George R. Goodman, as follows:

Hewn out of the stonework outside Catholic churches, one can sometimes see four curious figures which
. . . are variously described as representing the four
evangelists or the four living creatures mentioned in
the Apocalypse and Ezekiel. Actually, they are merely
the four points of the compass, and have been adopted from the Zodiac, in which they are known as the
four fixed signs, and are three months apart. They are
Leo the Lion, Taurus the Bull, Aquarius the Water-
Bearer and Scorpio, also known as the Eagle.
According to tradition the lion represents Shem, the
Lion of Judah, and the Semitic race. The Bull symbol-
izes Egypt and the land of Ham. Aquarius is said to
represent the mythical Noah and the remnants of the
Atlanteans, the Adamic race, driven by a catastropical
flood to the four quarters of the globe. And Scorpio or
the Eagle, belongs to Japheth who is alleged to have
traveled north, thus becoming the father of the Aryan
race (Goodman, *The Freethinker*, Vol. 85, p. 186).

In the eighteenth century Viscount Bolingbroke, Charles F.
Dupuis, and Count Volney discussed and wrote about the myth
theory of Christian origins. In the early nineteenth century this

propaganda was continued in England by the Reverend Robert Taylor. Reverend Taylor preached sermons in which he claimed that the Christian Savior was the Sun and that the story of his life was nothing more than the allegory of the passage of the solar orb through the twelve signs of the zodiac. As a result, Reverend Taylor was called the "Devil's Chaplain" and was sentenced to two years in jail for blasphemy. Taylor was an ordained minister, a surgeon, and a graduate of Cambridge University, but this did not save him from persecution. A Frenchman named Perez wrote a pamphlet to refute the Mythicists. As far as we know this tract was never translated into English, but a good digest of it was made by Herbert Cutner, whom I cite:

> It was a Frenchman called Perez who, early last century decided to annihilate the Sun Myth as applied to Jesus. He wrote a pamphlet which is often quoted . . . but few persons appear to have read it. Here then are some of the points it makes: First of all take the word "Napoleon." It is practically the same as "Apollon" or "Apollo," but if we take the spelling of his name as it appears on the column in the Place Vein-dome, *Neopoleon,* the prefix *Ne* which is Greek is a participle of affirmation, shows that Napoleon is the true Apollo or the Sun Bonaparte, his other name, really is *"bon* part" that is, the good part of the day — the sun giving us the good part, or daylight, and the moon and stars, the bad part — the Night or Darkness.

> Apollo was born on Delos, in the Mediterranean, while Napoleon was also born on a Mediterranean island, Corsica. Apollo was an Egyptian deity, so, of course, we can understand Napoleon going to Egypt and being received with homage and admiration.

> Napoleon's mother was called Lititia, which means joy, that is joy at the dawn of light, or the break of day, when the sun rises or is born; but also note that Apollo's mother was called Leto, which is very much like Letitia. Apollo had three sisters called the Graces; Napoleon had three sisters, also famed for their beauty. He also had four brothers — who, of course, represent the four seasons of the year. Three of these brothers were kings — Spring reigning over

**Apollo**

flowers, Summer reigning over the harvest, and Autumn holding sway over fruits. And just as the three kings held their authority through Napoleon, so the three seasons get theirs from the Sun. And why was one of Napoleon's brothers not a King? Because he represents Winter, which does not reign over anything.

It may be asserted that at least Winter had an empire over cold and waste. Well, Napoleon's brother was invested with a principality when the Emperor's power was declining as the Sun's does in Winter. It was called *Canino,* a word derived from Cani, which means the whitened hair of old age — that is, Winter.

Napoleon had two wives, so had Apollo. Apollo was given the Earth and the Moon. By the Moon he had Horus. Napoleon also had just one son.

Napoleon had twelve Marshals, obviously the twelve signs of the Zodiac; he, like the Sun, after being victorious in the South, where it represents its highest powers had to go North. Here he had to retreat, that is, the Sun is driven back upon his traces, a sign which represents the retrogression of the sun in that part of the sphere. It surely is clear that the story of Napoleon's march into Russia and his retreat is based on the Sun being driven back as explained above.

Finally, the sun rises in the East and sets in the West. What more beautiful proof could be given of Napoleon coming from his eastern isle in the Mediterranean and setting (dying) in the West on the island of St. Helena? (Herbert Cutner, *Jesus: God, Man or Myth?,* pp. 194-196.)

The argument of Perez was no doubt clever, but it was pointless, nevertheless, for nobody doubts the historicity of Napoleon.

One of the greatest merits of Ernest Busenbark's *Symbols, Sex and the Stars,* is his splendid chapter on the death and re-birth of the Sun God. For the benefit of those who are unable to consult that work I have attempted to condense it in the words of the author. The publisher of the book gave me the permission to make free use of this material.

**Leto**

### *"Allegory of the Seasons"*

As the sun appears to recede southward in autumn,
the days in the northern hemisphere become shorter
and cooler, vegetation withers, fertility of the earth
ceases, the sun stands lower in the sky, its warmth
and brightness are diminished. Allegorically speaking, the hours and powers of Darkness are gradually
winning over the powers of Light. On December 22, in
north temperate latitudes, there are twice as many
hours of darkness as there are of daylight. For weeks
the sun has been growing weaker and weaker. Now is
the culminating point, the shortest day of the year. On
this day the sun reaches his farthest point southward.
In Babylonian mythology this point represented the
gates of the underworld, presided over by Nergal, the
prince of Darkness. In the Hercules myth, it represented the arrival of the sun at the Pillars of
Hercules, which marked the end of his journey. As the
sun sinks below the horizon on this date, the forces of
Darkness achieve their victory. But the supremacy of
Darkness is quickly challenged, because the virgin
goddess (Virgo) gives birth to a new sun which
replaces the dead god on the following day, and a new
cycle begins. For about three days the length of the
day seems to remain unchanged, then it gradually
lengthens. The birth of the sun was personified in
Egypt by Horus, the god of light and savior of the
world. On the inner walls of the holy of holies in the
Temple of Luxor, the birth of Horus is depicted in a
series of four scenes which are strikingly similar to
Christian representations of the Annunciation and
Immaculate Conception of Mary and the Birth and
Adoration of Jesus. (Busenbark, *Symbols, Sex and The
Stars,* p. 116.)

### *"Spring"*

For weeks after the winter solstice, the puny, newborn sun struggles against the powers of Darkness.
Myths present the youngster as growing up in obscurity or concealment. But as the weeks pass, the young
sun god gathers strength, rising higher and higher in
the sky, his brightness increasing rapidly until on

March 21, he emerges victorious. This is the day of the spring equinox, when the sun crosses the equator. It is the turning point, the day of his Passover or Crossification. Night and day are of equal length all over the world on this date, the sun rising at 6:00 a.m. and setting at 6:00 p.m. Now begins a period in which the hours of light exceed the hours of darkness, symbolized as the sun's resurrection from the Underworld (the lower signs of the zodiac) and with its regeneration, life and vegetation can continue; the young sun redeems the world from darkness. During the Aries (Lamb) age, Egyptians celebrated this season by sacrificing a lamb. Three days later they celebrated the resurrection of the young sun-god. The Jewish custom of killing the paschal lamb and celebrating the Passover is said to celebrate the Lord's passage over the houses in Egypt when he slaughtered all of the first-born children and animals of the Egyptians. There is little reason to doubt that, originally, the celebration was an ancient solar festival. With the rise of Christianity, the day and hour on which the Jews were commanded to sacrifice the lamb came to be observed as the day and hour at which Christ died on the cross, his Resurrection being celebrated on the third day following. (Busenbark, *Symbols, Sex and The Stars,* pp. 119-120.)

### *"Summer"*

On June 21, the longest day of the year, the youthful sun reaches the farthest point northward in the ecliptic. On this day the sun rises earlier and sets later than on any other day in the year. On June 21, the earth's North Pole is inclined 23-1/2 degrees toward the sun, and on December 21 this position is reversed, the North Pole then being inclined 23-1/2 degrees away from the sun. To the Babylonians the point of the summer solstice represented the gate of Nibbu, the domain of the god Anu, "the point beyond which no man can pass." It marks the very peak of the sun god's virility when he shines with maximum brilliance and heat. The culminating point is at the full moon which marks the day when the sun mates with Ishtar, the Great Mother Goddess. It also marks the beginning of the sun's decline, for having given freely of his energy to restore fertility to the earth, his powers begin to wane, that is, the length of the days soon begins to decrease. In Babylon both the marriage and the decline of Tammuz were celebrated but a few days apart. This was the significance of that statement of Gilgamesh in which he accused Ishtar of being an enchanter, a poisoner, and a sapper of virility. For his death the people of Babylon and other Chaldean cities were in the habit of mourning and fasting for forty days prior to the festival of Ishtar. (Busenbark, *Symbols, Sex and The Stars*, pp. 120-121.)

### *"Autumn"*

On September 23 the powers of Light and Darkness are again on even terms (day and night being of equal length) and the sun now begins its entry into the Underworld. In Babylonian astrology this period marked the entry of the sun into the six lower signs of the zodiac and the six unlucky or unfruitful months. It was also observed by important religious ceremonies as the time of judgment, the period when men's deeds on earth were weighed in the Balance and, on the Zodiac, was symbolized by a pair of scales. At this period the Babylonians solemnly celebrated the Festival of Lights with processions of citizens carrying torches to symbolically light the passage of the dead through the Underworld . . . After the autumn equinox, the dark powers steadily increase their mastery over the sun until the final episode on December 22, when the cycle ends with the sun's death and the birth of a new sun savior. . . Here the axis and equator form a cross on which is placed the Macro-cosmic man, pierced through the heart by a spear which strikes him at an angle of 23-1/2 degrees, the exact angle of inclination of the ecliptic on December 22 and June 21. (Busenbark, *Symbols, Sex and The Stars*, pp. 122-124.)

### *"What The Stars Reveal"*

In most ancient calendars the year began at the time of the Vernal Equinox, March 22. According to calculations of some astronomers, the sun rose in the sign of Aries at this season of the year, from about 2512 to 360 B.C. It was within this period that astrology, the zodiac, and the sun god myths reached complete development, though the first zodiacal signs were charted in the sky much earlier.

As the earth makes a complete revolution every twenty-four hours, all of the twelve signs or constellations follow each other through the sky with a new one rising over the eastern horizon every two hours. And, as the earth advances in its orbit around the sun, the sun appears to rise in a different sign each month.

During the Aries Age sunrise was in Cancer at the summer solstice, in Libra at the autumn equinox, and in Capricorn at the winter solstice. Several hours before sunrise on December 25, or about midnight, the sign of the Virgin rose above the horizon. This was the hour of the young god's birth. The sacrificial lamb (Aries) was in the horizon with the rising of the Virgin in the east. High in the western sky, in the sign of Taurus, stood Orion, the star of Horus. The three bright stars in the belt of Orion were the three magi, or kings. Directly across the sky from Orion is the Scorpion, which a myth says followed him, as indeed it does in the Zodiac. In Taurus is the constellation of Columba, the dove, symbol of the Virgin and the Holy Ghost. At the feet of the Virgin is the herdsman Bootes. Within the sign of Taurus there is also a small group of stars called the stable (Auriga). This is the same Stable of Augeas, which Hercules mythically cleansed as his sixth labor, and Justin Martyr proudly boasted that Christ was born on the very day when the sun takes his birth in the Stable of Augeas in the sign of the Goat (Capricorn). It also agrees with the tradition that the sun god was born in a stable or cave (caves or niches carved in the rocks being sometimes used as stables) . . . In the sign of Scorpio is the small constellation of Aquila, the eagle. This bird was identified with the Greek god Zeus, the Hindu Krishna, the Hebrew Jahweh, and was one of the four animals mentioned in Ezekiel's mystic vision. The other animals are the bull (Taurus), lion (Leo), and man (Aquarius). During the Taurus Age the four bright stars Aldebaran, Regulus, Antares, and Fomalhaut in these signs, that is, Taurus, Leo, Scorpio, and Aquarius, marked the four cardinal periods of the year.

In the Aries Age, Capricorn was followed in January by the sign of Aquarius. The principal festival now marking this period is Epiphany, commemorating Christ's baptism and assumption of the Holy Spirit. It is the essence of symbolism that like qualities go together; therefore, when we read that the baptism of Christ by John the Baptist occurred on January 6, the event falls just where we should expect to find it, in

Aquarius, the Waterman. January 6 was observed in Egypt as the day of Nilos, when the water was said to be at its purest. Epiphanius wrote that this was the season when water was withdrawn from the river and stored not only in Egypt but in many other countries. In some places springs and rivers were said to turn into wine on this day. From this tradition a myth developed to the effect that Bacchus (Dionysus) turned water into wine at this very time of year; and, by one of those "coincidences" which are to be found so frequently in the Scriptures, the turning of water into wine at the marriage in Cana was the first miracle of Jesus. Two centuries after Epiphanius, Chrysostom commanded that the water be blessed and drawn from the rivers at the baptismal feast. In Roman Catholic communities priests still bestow blessings on rivers and other bodies of water at this season of the year, the practice doubtless being derived from the ancient Egyptian custom. (Busenbark, *Symbols, Sex and The Stars,* pp. 125-127.)

We have heard people say that since historical events are dated B.C. and A.C. or A.D., then there must have been an historical Jesus. Of course, this chronological scheme proves no such thing. Unitarians have eliminated the miraculous elements in the Gospel and then proceeded to accept the rest of narrative as ground for the biography of the man Jesus. This is entirely uncritical. In the words of Massey:

> The worst foes of the truth have ever been, and still are, the rationalizers of the Mythos, such as the Unitarians. They have assumed the human history as the starting point, and accepted the existence of a personal founder of Christianity as the one initial and fundamental fact. They have done their best to humanize the divinity of the Mythos, by discharging the supernatural and miraculous element, in order that the narrative might be accepted as history. Thus they have lost the battle from the beginning, by fighting it on the wrong ground. (Massey, *Lectures,* p. 23)

Joseph McCabe was an aggressive rationalist, but he vigorously opposed the arguments of Robertson, Massey, and the other mythicists:

I conclude only that it is more reasonable to believe in the historicity of Jesus. There is no parallel in history to the sudden growth of a myth and its conversion into a human personage in one generation. Moreover, to these early Christians Jesus is not primarily a teacher. A collection of wise teachings might in time get a mythical name attached to it — though why the name Jesus is attached to it is hard to see — and the myth might in further time become a real person. But from the earliest moment that we catch sight of Christians in history the essence of their belief is that Jesus was an incarnation, in Judea, of the great God of the universe. The supreme emphasis is on the fact that he assumed a human form and shed human blood on a cross. So it seems to me far more reasonable, far more scientific, far more consonant with the facts of religious history which we know, to conclude that Jesus was a man who was gradually turned into a God. (Joseph McCabe, *The Story of Religious Controversy,* Boston: Stratford Co., 1929, p. 228.)

The birth of Jesus Christ has been set at Christmas and his death and resurrection at Easter. But up to the fourth century, the birth of the Christian Savior was celebrated on the sixth of January. The reason why it was changed to December 25 was as follows:

Certain it is that the winter solstice, which ancients erroneously assigned to the twenty-fifth of December, was celebrated in antiquity as the birthday of the Sun, and that festal lights or fires were kindled on this joyful occasion. Our Christmas festival is nothing but a continuation under a Christian name of this old solar festivity; for the ecclesiastical authorities saw fit, about the end of the third or the beginning of the fourth century, arbitrarily to transfer the nativity of Christ from the sixth of January to the twenty-fifth of December, for the purpose of diverting to their Lord the worship which the heathen had hitherto paid on that day to the sun. (Frazer, *The New Golden Bough,* p. 722.)

Everyone knows that Easter is a roving date in the calendar, since it is the first Sunday after the first full moon after the Vernal Equinox (the beginning of Spring). Easter, therefore, cannot be the date of the death of any historical personage. Two dates are given in the New Testament for the time of the crucifixion, namely: the 14th and 15th of the month of Nisan. Why this discrepancy? The true explanation was given by Gerald Massey:

> The Synoptics say that Jesus was crucified on the 15th of the month of Nisan. John affirms that it was on the 14th of the month. This serious rift runs through the very foundation! As human history it cannot be explained. But there is an explanation possibly, which, if accepted proves the Mythos. The crucifixion (or Crossing) was, and still is, determined by the full moon of Easter. This, in the lunar reckoning, would be on the 14th in a month of twenty-eight days; in the solar month of thirty days it was reckoned to occur on the 15th of the month. Both unite, and the rift closes in proving the Crucifixion to have been astronomical, just as it was in Egypt, where the two dates can be identified. (Massey, *Lectures*, p. 6.)

It is the tradition among orthodox Christians that Jesus Christ was buried on Good Friday and arose from the tomb on Easter Sunday. There are no historical data for this belief, but it may be easily explained mythologically. This was done by the English scholar, Godfrey Higgins:

> The Gospels all agree that Jesus rose on the Sunday morning, and pointedly and unnecessarily, unless there was a particular meaning intended to be conveyed say *very early before daylight*. But the tradition is, that he rose the moment after midnight of the second day. At Rome, at some of the churches, the ceremonies begin at this time, and in Syria, in commemoration of the resurrection of Adonis; and now in the same place and at that same time, the ceremonies of the resurrection of Jesus Christ begin to be celebrated.
>   If the calculations of the mythos be commenced on the moment of the conjunction of the sun and moon, and the neros lasts 600 years, twenty-eight hours, one minute and forty-two seconds, there must be, to make it come right, an intercalation in every neros or 600 years, of $28^h1^m$ 52$^s$. Then this will make the life of the sun end precisely in such a manner, in such a part of a day, as will be $28^h$ $1^m$ 41$^s$ before a third day begins,

making it go one second into the third day to complete the $28^h$ $1^m$ $52^s$. Thus the reason why he is in the grave, as it is called, three days, is apparent. The millennium cycle was supposed to have begun at such an hour and minute of the day on which the sun first entered Taurus at the vernal equinox, as would make the eighth cycle or neros end at an hour which may be found by close examination of the history. It is said that Jesus was buried before the Sabbath began; that would be before six on Friday evening. Then if he were the shortest time possible in the grave, to be consistent with history, he would be there from six to twelve, or the last six hours of Friday, twenty-four hours of Saturday, and say one second of Sunday, and he would rise very early, as the text says on Sunday morning. This makes one day, six hours, in the grave. Now what is the time necessary to be intercalated to correct the error to a second time? It is one day, four hours, one minute, forty-two seconds. Then the authors of the mythos were in error, the difference $1^d$ $4^h$ $1^m$ $42^s$ and $1^d$ $6^h$ $0^m$ $0^s$. This is $1^h$ $58^m$ $18^s$, which on 7421 lunations, the number there are in the cycle, makes an error in the moon's period of somewhat less than one second. This, I think, is bringing the matter pretty nearly to a point . . . By calculating backwards and allowing a day and part of a day for the error every six hundred years, the calculators made in the eight neros, nine, but not ten days: thus 9 x 72 = 648 + 2160 = 2808 + 360 = 3168 - 4 = 3164. This seems to me to be a real arithmetic proof of the truth of my explanation of the three days, or, more correctly, the day and part of a day in the grave.

From:

| | | |
|---|---|---|
| Taurus to Aries | 2160 | 3164 |
| Aries to Pisces | 2160 | 2160 |
| Pisces to Jesus | | |
| Christ | 360 | 5324 |
| 9x72 | 648 | |
| | 5328 | |
| | -4 | |
| | 5324 | |

The history of the sun, I repeat, is the history of Jesus Christ. The sun is born on the 25th of December, the birthday of Jesus Christ. The first and greatest of the labors of Jesus Christ is his victory over the serpent, the evil principle, or the devil. In his first labor Hercules strangled the serpent, as did Krishna, Bacchus, etc. This is the sun triumphing over the powers of hell and darkness; and, as he increases, he prevails, till he is crucified in the heavens, or is decussated in the form of a cross (according to Justin Martyr) when he passes the equator at the vernal equinox. But before he rises he is dead for one day and about four hours. This is nearly the time necessary to be intercalated every six hundred years, to make the calculation come right; at the beginning of the third day he rises again to life and immortality. The twelve labors of Hercules are his labors in passing through the signs of the zodiac, which are so similar to the history of Jesus Christ, as to induce the revered, pious, and orthodox Parkhurst to declare them types of what the real Savior was to do and suffer. These celestial images are what induced the learned Alphonso the Great to declare, that the whole history of Jesus Christ might be read in the stars. (*Anacalypsis*, Vol. II, pp. 143-145.)

Historical Christianity is based on the four Gospels. These works were supposedly written by the four Evangelists: (2) Mark, (2) Matthew, (3) Luke, and (4) John. The Gospel of John has no value as an historical document. It was written as an interpretation of the mission of Jesus in terms of Hellenistic metaphysics and Alexandrine theology. The other three Gospels are called the Synoptics, because they are a synopsis of an earlier source document. These three Gospels were written sometime between 65 and 95 A.D. E. Mark, it seems, appeared between 65 and 70 A.D.; Matthew between 70 and 75 AD.; and Luke between 78 and 93 A.D. None of these writings have any historical value, and their supposed authors never existed. The four Evangelists, Matthew, Luke, John and Mark were myth duplicates of the four Sons of Horus of ancient Egypt. These were Amset, Tuamutef, Gebhsennuf and Hapi. They were the four corner constellations of the Zodiac. So the four so-called gospel writers were just as mythical as were their writings. God mythology cannot be transmuted into bad history.

Besides the canonical Gospels, which are contained in the New Testament, there were over one hundred Apocyphal Gospels. Of these now only twenty-three books survive. The names of these are here listed, with a few brief commentaries on several:

## I
### The Gospel of the Birth of Mary

There are several versions of this gospel. One version deals mainly with the story of the birth of the Virgin Mary. In another account Jesus is said not to have been descended from David, but was a Levite, the descent being traced through his mother, Mary. More than one version, of Gnostic tendency, held that Jesus did not become the Christ until after his baptism.

## II
### The Protevangelion

This work was said to have been written by James, the brother of the Lord Jesus, and the first Bishop of Jerusalem. This gospel alleges that Joseph was accused of corrupting Mary before his marriage to her, and that both he and Mary were tried on this charge and that they gave evidence concerning the miraculous birth of Jesus.

## III
### The First Gospel of the Infancy of Jesus Christ

This gospel was published about the same time as were the Canonical Gospels. In it is an element of Gnosticism, but it was well regarded by Eusebius, Athanasius, and Chrysostom. It was also popular among the Nestorians, a heretical Christian sect. Here we are regaled with a number of miracles and marvels attributed to the Christ-child while sojourning in Egypt. Joseph, the foster-father of Jesus, was a carpenter. On one occasion he sawed off a piece of board too short and the boy Jesus obligingly stretched out the board to its correct length. He, at one time, mixed up the dyes of a cloth dyer and then by a miracle changed all the clothes to the color desired by their owner. Another miracle was the curing of a newly-married man of impotence. He also cured Judas Iscariot, when a boy, of a devil which had possessed him, and which left him in the form of a dog. The youthful Jesus met a man who had been bewitched into a mule and proceeded to change him back to human shape. As a school-boy Jesus and his schoolfellows shaped images of animals of clay, and Jesus brought these images to life. In this curious book are also stories of several miracles performed by the Virgin Mary.

## IV
### Thomas' Gospel of The Infancy of Jesus Christ

Only four chapters of this gospel have survived. It contains stories of several miracles said to have been performed by Jesus.

## V
### The Epistles of Jesus Christ and Abgarus, King of Edessa

The first letter was alleged to have been written by King Abgarus inviting Jesus to visit him at Edessa, in Mesopotamia. He wanted Jesus to cure him of an illness.

The second letter, from Jesus to the king, declined the invitation but promised to send a disciple to cure the illness.

These Epistles were considered as genuine by Eusebius, who wrote early in the fourth century. Some pastors in Great Britain, at a later date, attempted to have them admitted into the Canon but were unsuccessful.

## VI
### The Gospel of Nicodemus, or The Acts of Pontius Pilate

This gospel was probably written near the end of the second century and widely used by the end of the third century. This work was allegedly a part of the official records of Pilate, supposedly found among the Roman archives in Jerusalem. Actually, it was a pious fraud, concocted by a Christian propagandist. We read that Jesus was accused before Pontius Pilate of being a magician and a bastard. Numerous witnesses testified to the veracity of the miraculous cures performed by Jesus. Among the dead saints who arose from the grave at the time of the crucifixion, two told of their adventures in Hell, and how there they met Adam and Isaiah. Jesus also visited Hell. Beelzebub, Prince of Hell, denounced Satan, the keeper of the infernal regions, for the crucifixion of Jesus, and Jesus gave Beelzebub dominion over Satan. Jesus was pictured as leading Adam by the hand, followed by other saints, in an exodus from Hell. The Archangel Michael then conducted the party of Heaven. The saints Enoch and Elijah were not in this group, since they had entered Heaven without having gone to Hell.

203

## XXI
### The First Book (or Visions) of Hermas

## XXII
### The Second Book (or Commands) of Hermas

## XXIII
### The Third Book (or Similitudes) of Hermas

There were many other Apocryphal works which were pronounced spurious, and hence ceased to be published. One of them was *The Acts* of *Thomas*. The Apostle Judas Thomas was said to have been the first Christian Missionary to India. An interesting story of his adventures has been related:

> When Thomas arrives in India he is brought before the King, and being questioned as to his knowledge of mason's and carpenter's work, professes great skill in either department. The King asks him if he can build him a palace. He replies that he can, and makes a plan which is approved of. He is then commissioned to build the palace, and is supplied abundantly with money for the work which, however, he says he cannot begin until the winter months. The King thinks this strange, but acquiesces. When the King goes away Thomas, instead of building, employs himself in the preaching of the Gospel, and spends all the money on the poor. After a time the King sends to know how the work is going on. Thomas sends back word that the palace is finished all but the roof, for which he must have more money; and this supplied accordingly, and is spent by Thomas on the widows and orphans as before. At length the King returns to the city, and when he makes inquiry about the palace he learns that Thomas has never done anything but go about preaching, giving alms to the poor, and healing diseases. He seemed to be a magician, yet he never took money for his cures; lived on bread and water, with salt, and had but one garment. The King in great anger, sent for Thomas. "Have you built the palace? Let me see it." "Oh, you can't see it now, but you will

see it when you go out of this world." Enraged by being thus mocked, the King committed Thomas to prison, until he could devise some terrible form of death for him. But that same night the King's brother died, and his soul was taken up by the angels to see all the heavenly habitations. They asked him in which he would like to dwell. But when he saw the palace which Thomas had built he desired to dwell in none but that. When he learned that it belonged to his brother he begged and obtained leave that he might return to life in order that he might buy it from him. So, as they were putting the grave clothes on the body, it returned to life. He sent for the King, whose love for him he knew, and implored him to sell him the palace. But when the King learned the truth about it he refused to sell the mansion he hoped to inhabit himself, but consoled his brother with the promise that Thomas, who was still alive, should build him a better one. The two brothers then received instruction and were baptised. (Rhys, *Shaken Creeds,* pp. 70-71.)

In reading the Gospel accounts of the early life and ministry of Jesus, we find that nothing of any certainty was known about his birth, childhood, and early manhood. The Mark Gospel and that of St. John say nothing of a virgin birth but start their story with the ministry of Jesus. The Gospels of Luke and Matthew deal with the early years of the Savior, and the writers disagree with each other in so many instances as to make their accounts of no historical value. Neither story appeared before 100 A.D. , and it is not known who wrote them. Two birthplaces are given for the Lord Jesus, Bethlehem and Nazareth. Bethlehem was situated in Judea, about five miles south of Jerusalem. Nazareth is a considerable distance north of Jerusalem. Since nobody can be born in two places, then either one or both accounts are false.

The Matthew Narrator said that Jesus was born in a house, but according to Luke his first birthplace was a stable. Another tradition told of his birth in a cave. The cave story is obviously mythological and so is that about the stable. The Egyptologist, Sir Arthur Weigall, was a member of the Church of England and firmly believed in the historicity of Jesus, but he was compelled to admit that the Markan and Lukan stories of the birth of the Savior were mythological, for he declared that:

Firstly, as regards the cave; the cave shown at Bethlehem as the birthplace of Jesus was actually a rock shrine in which the god Tammuz or Adonis was worshipped as the early Christian Father, Jerome tells us; and its adoption as the scene of the birth of our Lord was one of those frequent instances of the taking over by Christians of a pagan sacred site. The propriety of this appropriation was increased by the fact that the worship of a god in a cave was a commonplace in paganism: Apollo, Cybele, Demeter, Herakles, Hermes, Mithra and Poseidon were all adored in caves; Hermes, the Greek *Logos,* being actually born of Maia in a cave, and Mithra being rock-born.

Then as regards the stable: St. Luke says that when the child was born Mary wrapped him in swaddling clothes and laid him in a manger *(phatne),* that is to say a rough trough, like the Greek *liknon,* which was a sort of basket used either for hay or as an actual cradle, somewhat as the manger is represented in Botticelli's picture of the Nativity. The author of the Gospel of St. Luke, however, was here drawing upon Greek mythology; for the god Hermes was wrapped in swaddling clothes when he was born and placed in a *liknon,* or manger-basket. So also was the god Dionysus, who in Bithynia, gave his name to the month beginning at our Christmas, and who. . .was closely related to the popular conception of Jesus. (Weigall, *The Paganism in our Christianity,* pp. 51-52.)

As we have seen, December 25th, Christmas Day, could not have been the birthday of an historical Jesus. This has been conceded by many eminent Christian scholars. Again I cite Weigall:

I may add that the time of the year of which Jesus was born is completely unknown, the date of our Christmas Day, December 25th, having been adopted by the Church only in the Fourth Century A.D., this being the traditional date of the birth of the sun-god. . . Nothing, in fact, is known historically, about the early years of our Lord. All that can be said is that He was the son of a carpenter named Joseph and of his wife, probably called Mary, who seem to have lived at Nazareth, or the neighboring hamlet of Bethlehem.

These two had at least seven children, there being five sons — Jesus, James, Joses, Judas and Simon, and two or more daughters whose names are not known; and we may therefore picture our Lord as growing up with his brothers and sisters in the usual rough manner of a middle-class native household, but gradually detaching Himself from them as his religious consciousness developed. *(The Paganism in our Christianity,* pp. 53-54.)

In the supposed biographies of Jesus in the Bible only the early and late years of his life could be discussed because there was a blank period of eighteen years between the ages of twelve and thirty. I have referred to that fact earlier in this essay. Most Christian writers don't even mention it since any explanation of it would be pure speculation from their viewpoint. We have been informed that Jesus Christ was crucified and that he afterwards rose from the dead and finally ascended to heaven. The Christian Father Irenaeus wrote a book, *Against Heresies,* about 180 A.D., and in this work he mentioned that there were in his day Christians who denied that Jesus was crucified. They claimed that Jesus metamorphosed himself and that Simon of Cyrene took his place on the cross. As for Jesus, he lived on for many years and died as an old man. Some scholars have regarded this story as a forgery. But this is hard to believe. As an English authority remarked:

> It is quite impossible to imagine a Christian forger would have deliberately inserted a statement to the effect that Jesus died an old man with the Divine Authority of the Gospels against him. On the other hand, one can easily imagine that a forger, horrified at the statement of Irenaeus, thought it better served the Faith to add a sentence of his own that the Christ was crucified by Pontius Pilate. (Cutner, *Jesus — God, Man or Myth?,* p. 102.)

In the Gospel of John, Jesus has been shown as carrying the cross on the way to the crucifixion, while in the Synoptics the cross-bearer was Simon of Cyrene. According to Mark, Jesus was crucified at the third-hour (9:00 a.m.), but Luke gave the time as the sixth hour (12:00 noon), whereas John stated that at noontime Jesus had not yet been sentenced to death, so it must have been later that day. What are we to believe? In dealing with the Gospel Myths, in a scholarly study J. M. Robertson wrote a passage both brief and bril-

liant on the cross-bearing by Simon of Cyrene. Since this great
work is now out of print, I cite in full the section to which I refer:

> Another item in the gospel story can with some
> degree of probability be traced to an artistic repre-
> sentation of a pagan myth. One of the subsidiary
> labors of Hercules was the setting up of two pillars at
> Gades (Cadiz) to mark the boundaries of Europe and
> Libya. Here the cult of Herakles combines with that
> of his Phoenician double, the Sun-God Melkarth, wor-
> shipped at Gades, of whose mythus the Samson leg-
> end in the Hebrew Bible is a variant. The two pillars
> (represented in the Hebrew as in the Phoenician tem-
> ples), are simply ancient symbol-limits of the course
> of the sun in the heavens; and, as usual we have a
> variety of legends in the different mythologies to
> explain them. In the Samson legend they occur twice,
> figuring as the gateposts of Gaza, which the hero car-
> ries off; in another as the two pillars of the Philistine
> hall, between which the shorn and blinded hero sits in
> his captivity; Samson here being the winter sun, weak
> and rayless; at the end, of course, and therefore touch-
> ing at least one pillar. Now just as Samson in one
> story carries the pillars, so did Herakles, as became
> his strength, carry his pillars to their places; even as
> in the Tyrian form of the legend he dies at the very
> place where he has set them up. And in ancient art he
> was actually represented carrying the two pillars in
> such a way under his arms that they formed exactly a
> cross. Here, perhaps, we have the origin of the myth
> of Jesus carrying his own cross to the place of execu-
> tion. Christian art has always represented him as
> staggering under the load, as even Herakles stoops
> with the weight of his columns. Singularly enough,
> the three synoptics substitute for Jesus as cross-bear-
> er one Simon, a man of Cyrene, coming from the coun-
> try — a way of suggesting perhaps, that he was
> strong. Cyrene is in Libya, the legendary scene, as we
> saw, of the pillar-carrying of Herakles; and in
> Palestine Simon, Semo or Sem, was actually a God-
> name, representing the ancient Sun-God Semesh,
> identified with Baal, with whose mythus that of
> Samson unquestionably connects. And the God Semo
> or Simon was especially worshipped in Samaria. That

district, lying between Galilee and Judea, must at an early period have tended to affect the Jesuist legend; and in the third and fourth gospels, the Founder visits the region and wins converts in it. What more likely than a representation of the Sun-Hero Simon (so recognized by the many Jews settled in Greek-speaking countries), carrying his pillars crosswise, should come to figure as that of a man Simon carrying a cross? The two versions of the cross-bearing satisfy us that the story is a myth: is any hypothesis more probable than that Simon the Cyrenian's task is a variant of that of the Cyrenian Simon-Herakles? (Roberson, *Christianity and Mythology*, pp. 368-369.)

The mother of Jesus, according to John, was a spectator of the Crucifixion, but this was not so if we believe the other Evangelists, who, however, named Magdalene as being among those present. In what year was Jesus allegedly crucified? According to holy writ it occurred during the rule of Pontius Pilate and when Caiaphas was a High Priest of the Jews; or anytime between 26 and 36 A.D. One hundred so-called Christian authorities attempted to name the year in which Christ was crucified; twenty-three gave the year 29, eighteen said the year 30 was correct, nine gave the year 31, seven settled for the year 32, thirty-seven concluded that the year 33 was right, and six stood up for 36 A.D.

The glaring contradictions of the story of the Resurrection have to be read to be appreciated. If we follow John, Mary Magdalene was the lone visitor to the tomb on the first Easter morn. Matthew said that Mary Magdalene was accompanied by the other Mary. Mark names Mary Magdalene and Mary the mother of James and Salome. Luke asserted that it was Mary Magdalene, Mary the Mother of James, Joanna, and some other women. These women, stated Mark, came at sunrise, but John said that they arrived when it was not dark. When these pilgrims arrived the tomb was closed according to Matthew, but open if we consult Luke, who stated that the stone covering the tomb had been rolled away. The women met an angel, if we listen to Matthew; Mark said they saw a young man; Luke recorded two men; and John asserted that the women observed two angels. Walter Cassels in his scholarly study *Supernatural Religion,* studied the Resurrection narratives in detail and then concluded that since there were no witnesses to this alleged event then we must dismiss it as being an historical happening. If there was no crucifixion and no resurrection, then there was also no ascension. This has caused considerable embarrassment to educated and intelligent Christians. Some of the attempts to explain away the traditional beliefs have been quite ingenious. Sir Arthur Weigall has surmised that Jesus did not die on the cross, that he was taken into the tomb still alive and then revived by some friends and spirited away. In the words of Weigall:

> Jesus had not passed beyond recall upon the cross, but that having sunk into a condition indistinguishable from death, He was carried to the sepulchre, where He recovered, and was perhaps given somebody's clothing to wear, which led to His being mistaken for the gardener. In this case, the supposed angelic figures seen by the two Marys would have been mortal men who had helped our Lord during the night. In support of this theory it is to be observed that He had not been much hurt by being Crucified. It was not the custom to drive nails through the feet, for the victim usually stood upon a block projecting from the cross; and the Gospel of St. John speaks of His hands being wounded but not his feet. The victim's arms were generally tied to the crossbeam, and if the hands were nailed it was only an added insult, a small nail being driven through the flesh of each hand, between the fingers, without causing a serious wound. A soldier had pricked our Lord's side to see if he were dead, but this wound also might have been slight; and in other respects He would have been little worse for the short exposure on the cross ....

> The Gospel stories then proceed to tell us how He appeared to His disciples, and they are emphatic that he was alive and not merely a spirit.... He was alive, saying: "Handle me and see for a spirit would not have flesh and bones as you see I have." He then asked them, as well a hungry outlaw might, whether they had anything for him to eat; and they gave Him some fish and honey, after eating which He led them as far as Bethany, two miles from Jerusalem, and then departed...

> St. Paul says that five hundred persons saw him at one time. But the last appearance to be described in detail is that which is recorded in the Gospel of St. John, when, early one morning, the disciples who were

fishing in the Lake of Tiberias (the Sea of Galilee) saw Him on the shore, and he asked them for food. Obviously, this was no spirit: it was a man in hiding; and the last picture we have of Him shows Him cooking some fish over a fire out here in the open in the grey light of dawn . . . The orthodox Christian is entitled to say that the divine spiritual part of Him immediately ascended to God; but whether this occurred at once or not, in the end His mortal body must have died and returned to dust. (Weigall *The Paganism in Our Christianity,* pp. 97-101.)

The religions of the world may be divided into two main types: namely, the natural and the supernatural, or Atheistic and theistic. The great Western cults such as Judaism, Christianity, and Islam are theistic, since they are founded on the belief in a personal god. The great Eastern cults such as Buddhism, Confucianism, and Theosophy are Atheistic religions, since they are not based on the belief in a personal god. The theological god is personal, whereas the metaphysical god is nonpersonal. Many educated people in the Western World today are turning back to the wisdom of the ancients, who believed in a Great God who was not anthropomorphic but just a name for the Universe, the All in All which has neither beginning nor end. The Minor gods were symbols of the laws and forces of Nature. Such ideas are embraced in the African Traditional Religion and in the most advanced type of religion in the Western World, which has been called by the Rev. Professor Thomas Altizer and the Rev. Dr. Paul Van Buren, Christian Atheism. Atheists have been popularly considered as anti-religious people. But many Atheists are and have been Spiritualists and Theosophists, and are not these people religious? Madam Alexandra David Neel lived for many years among the mystics of Tibet. From a Christian viewpoint these people are Atheists, but they certainly are not without religion. Madam David-Neel has said that:

To present to Westerners a perfectly clear and complete idea of the mysticism of the Tibetans is almost impossible . . . In the West a mystic is a devout person — of a very superior type, granted, but always essentially a believer, the worshiper of a god. On the contrary, the Tibetan mystic will probably be regarded by many Occidentals as an Atheist. If we call him by such a name, however, we must guard against attributing to the term those feelings and ideas which it connotes in Western lands. In countries under Christian influence the Atheist for centuries past has been a rare exception, a kind of demonical character appearing in the flock of faithful believers. Even in these days he appears before the imagination of many as a rebel confronting Faith and Religion in a theatrical attitude of denial and challenge. There is nothing like this in Tibet, where the idea of a supreme personal God has never held sway. (Alexandra David-Neel, *Initiations and Initiates of Tibet*, pp. 11-12.)

Professor John S. Mbiti is an authority on African religions, and he tells us that:

As far as is known, there are no images or physical representations of God by African peoples: this being one clear indication that they consider him to be a Spiritual Being. The fact that He is invisible also leads many to visualize Him as spiritual rather than physical. One of the most explicit descriptions of God as Spirit occurs in a traditional Pygmy hymn which says:

In the beginning was God
Today is God
Tomorrow will be God.
Who can make an image of God?
He has no body.
He is a word, which comes out
    of your mouth.
That word! It is no more,
It is past, and still it lives!
So is God.

In a Shona traditional hymn God is addressed as the Great Spirit who piles up rocks to make mountains, causes branches to grow and gives rain to mankind. Thus, God is pictured as an active and creative Spirit. It is particularly as Spirit that God is incomprehensible. So the Ashanti rightly refers to him as the fathomless Spirit, since no human mind can measure Him, no intellect comprehend or grasp him . . . So God confronts men as the mysterious and incomprehensible and beyond human vocabulary. This is part of the essential nature of God. (John S. Mbiti, *African Religions and Philosophy,* pp. 44-45.)

The god of the theologians is personal; the god of the philosophers is non-personal. This difference, not being apparent to many people, has caused a considerable confusion of thought. When Sir James Jeans said that he believed that god was a Great Mathematician whose symbol was the square root of minus one, the unit of the system of imaginary numbers, he certainly was not talking about the anthropomorphical god of the orthodox Christians. Many Christians denounce Paganism as false religion. If this is correct, then Christianity is also false, for it is of pagan origin, and if one is not true, then neither is the other. Outstanding thinkers such as the philosopher, Spinoza; the astronomer, Professor Fred Hoyle; and the Egyptologist, Dr. Margaret Murray, have said that god is just another name for nature, or the Universe.

These ideas are not exactly new, for a great French scholar expressed some of them in the late eighteenth century. I refer to Charles Francis Dupuis. This scholar wrote voluminously, but a good one-volume edition of his best writings was published under the title *Dupuis' Explanation of an Apocalyptical Work,* translated by Gilbert Vale. On god and his worship Dupuis wrote as follows:

The word *God* appears destined to express the universal and eternally active force which gives motion to everything in nature, according to the laws of a constant and admirable harmony which develops itself in the different forms taken by organized matter, which intermingles with everything animates everything, and which seems to be one unallied in its infinitely varied modifications, and to belong but to itself. Such is the living force which the universe, or that regular assemblage of all bodies, which an eternal chain links together, encloses within itself, and which a perpetual motion majestically impels in the bosom of boundless space and time. It is in this vast and marvelous *ensemble* that man, from the moment he wished to reason upon the causes of his existence and of his preservation, as well as upon those of the various effects which are born and destroy themselves around him, ought first to have placed that sovereignly cause, which makes everything spring forth, and in the bosom of which everything reenters again to return out of it, by a succession of new generations and under different forms. . .

Behold, the great God, the first, or rather, the only God, which has manifested himself to man through the veil of the matter he animates, and which forms the immense body of the Divinity. Such is the sense of the sublime inscription of the temple of Sais: "I am all which has been, all which is, all which shall be, and no mortal has yet raised the veil which covers me. . .He who sees the world sees God, as much as man can see him; as he who sees the body of a man and his movements, sees the man as much as he can be seen, though the principle of his movements, of his life, and of his intelligence remains concealed under the envelope that the hand touches and that the eye perceives. It is the same with the sacred body of the Divinity or the Universe — God. *(The Universe: God and His Worship,* pp. 1-4.)

On the worship rendered to nature Dupuis expressed himself thusly:

It is no longer by reasoning that we will endeavor to prove that the universe and its parts considered as so many portions of the Great Cause or Great Being, ought to have attracted the attention and the homage of mortals. It is by facts and by an abstract of the religious history of all nations that we are enabled to demonstrate that what ought to have been, has effectively been, and that all mankind of every country from the most remote antiquity, have had no other gods than the natural gods, that is today the world and the moon, the planets, the fixed stars, the elements, and in general everything bearing the characteristic of cause and perpetuity in nature . . . Cheremon and the most learned priests of Egypt were persuaded, the same as Pliny, that nothing except the world, or except the visible cause, ought to be admitted, and they supported their opinion by that of the most ancient Egyptians who only recognized, they say, four gods, the sun, the moon, the planets, the stars comprising the zodiac, and all those which, by their rising or setting mark the division of the signs, their interior subdivisions, the horoscope and the stars which preside over it, and which they name the powerful chiefs of heaven. They affirmed, that the Egyptians, considering the sun as a great God, the architect and moderator of the universe, explained not only the fable of Osiris, but moreover all their other religious fables generally by the stars and the play of their motions, by their apparition, their disapparition; by the phases of the moon, by the increase or the diminution of its light, by the progressive march of the sun, by the division of the heavens and of time into their two great parts, the one belonging to the day, the other to the night, by the Nile; in short, by the action of physical causes. They are said to be the gods-sovereign, arbiters of fate, that our fathers have honored with sacrifices, and to whom they have raised images . . . It was in honor of the orb which gives us light, that they built the town of the sun, or Heliopolis, and a temple in which they placed the statue of this god. It was a gift, and represented a beardless young man, with his arm raised, a whip in his right hand, in the attitude of a charioteer; in his left hand were the thunder bolts and ears of corn. It was thus they designated the power, and altogether the beneficience of the god who lights the fires of the thunder, and who yields that which makes the harvest spring up and ripen. . . In short, the world, in the Egyptian system, was regarded as a great Divinity, composed of the assemblage of a crowd of gods, or partial causes, who were nothing else than the diverse members of the great body called the World or the Universe-God . . . The Ethiopians, progenitors of the Egyptians, placed in a burning climate, did not less adore the Divinity of the sun, and above all that of the moon, who presided over the nights, and whose wild freshness made them forget the scorching heat of the day. All of the Africans sacrificed to these two great divinities. It was in Ethiopia that was found the famous table of the sun. The Ethiopians who dwelt above Meroë admitted gods eternal and of an incorruptible nature, says Diodorus, such as the sun, the moon, and the whole universe. *(Universality of the Worship Rendered to Nature*, pp. 1-4.)

Of the animated and intelligent universe, we read:

It is right to consider in the universe all the affinities under which the ancients have considered it. They were very far from seeing in the world a machine without life and without intelligence, moved by a blind and necessary force. The greatest and soundest part of the philosophers thought that the universe eminently contained the principle of life and motion which nature had placed in themselves, because it existed eternally in nature, as in the abundant and teeming source, the results of which vivified and animated everything possessing life and intelligence . . . Men believed that the universe lived like man and like the other animals, or rather that those only lived because the universe, essentially animated, communicated to them for some instants an infinitely small portion of its eternal life which it poured into the gross and inert matter of the sublunary bodies. Did it withdraw that portion from them, the man and the animal died, and the universe alone, always living, circulated, by its perpetual motion, around the remains of their bodies, and organized new beings. (pp. 1-2.)

Cleanthes, who looked upon the universe as God, or as the universal and unproduced cause of all effects, gave to the world a soul and an intelligence, and it was to that intelligent soul that properly belonged the Divinity. God, according to him, established his principal seat in the ethereal substance, in that subtle and luminous element which circulates around the firmament, and which thence impregnates all the stars, who thus share the divine nature. (p. 3.)

Thus, the universe is one vast body, moved by one soul, governed and guided by one intelligence which have one extent, and which acts in all its parts, that is to say, in everything which exists, since nothing exists out of the universe, which is the assemblage of all things. (p. 4.)

The universe was then a unique God, composed of the assemblage of a crowd of gods, which concurred as partial causes in the total action, it exercises itself in itself and upon itself. Thus formed itself that great administration, one only in its wisdom and in its primitive force, but multiplied *ad infinitum* in its secondary agents, called gods, angels, genie, etc., and with which men believed they could treat as they treated

with the ministers and the agents of human adminis-
trations. (p. 13.)

Count Volney, who based *The Ruins of Empires* on the research of
Dupuis, concluded that both civilization and religion originated
among the African Ethiopians. In referring to the ancient kingdom
of Ethiopia, Volney observed that:

> There a people, now forgotten, discovered, while oth-
> ers were yet barbarians, the elements of the arts and
> sciences. A race of men, now rejected from society for
> their *sable skin and frizzled hair,* founded on the study
> of the laws of nature, those civil and religious systems
> which still govern the universe. *(The Ruins of Empires,*
> pp. 16-17.)

Peter Eckler in the publisher's preface to the work cited above
commented as follows:

> A voluminous note, in which standard authorities
> are cited, seems to prove that this statement is sub-
> stantially correct, and that we are in reality indebted
> to the ancient Ethiopians, to the fervid imagination of
> the persecuted and despised Negro, for the various
> religious systems now so highly revered by the differ-
> ent branches of both the Semitic and Aryan races. This
> fact, which is so frequently referred to in Mr. Volney's
> writings, may perhaps solve the questions as to the
> origin of all religions, and may even suggest a solution
> to the secret so long concealed beneath the flat nose,
> thick lips, and Negro features of the Egyptian Sphinx.
> It may also confirm that statement of Diodorus, that,
> "The Ethiopians conceive themselves as the inventors
> of divine worship, of festivals, of solemn assemblies, of
> sacrifices, and of every other religious practice."

That an imaginative and superstitious race of black
men should have invented and founded, in the dim
obscurity of past ages, a system of religious belief that
still enthralls the minds and clouds the intellects of
the leading representatives of modern theology — that
still clings to the thoughts, and tinges with its potential influences the literature and faith of the civilized
and cultured nations of Europe and America, is indeed

a strange illustration of the mad caprice of destiny, of the insignificant and apparently trivial causes that often produce the most grave and momentous results. (Volney *The Ruins of Empires,* pp. *iii* and *iv.*)

The conclusions of Count Volney were subsequently confirmed by Professor A. H. L. Heeren, General J. G. R. Forlong, Gerald Massey, Dr. Albert Churchward, and Lady Flora Lugard. The Ethiopian contributions to culture and mythology were best stated by the Scottish anthropologist, General J. G. R. Forlong, whom we cite:

It was undoubtedly Kushites who rendered possible the Aryan advance, and who played the part of a civilizing Rome thousands of years before Rome's birth. It was their vast mythology and strange legends that passed as Lord Bacon wrote, 'like light air into the flutes of Grecians, there to be modulated as best suited Grecian fancies. Indeed, it is manifest from many old writings, that it was their tales, myths, traditions and histories that lay at the base of the Western World's thought and legendary lore. These so impressed all subsequent races and entered so deeply and minutely into all Aryan mythologies that many writers now think Aryans can only claim to have added to the superstructure and complexion of Ethiopian myths and mythical history; and let us remember that active Aryan life and mythologies began at least 3000 years B.C. when high Asia . . . becoming too cramped for this race, they were pressing southward to India and Ariana and to the west generally. Then and there must Aryans have met with Ethiopian civilization, as did Semites, when these began to group themselves into nations about a thousand years later, or say 2000 B.C. They were all builders on old Kushite foundations. (J. G. R. Forlong, *Rivers of Life,* London: Bernard Quaritch, 1883, Vol. II, pp. 403-404.)

The sources and authorities mentioned and cited in this essay have been listed in the bibliography.

# Bibliography

Allen, Grant. *The Evolution of The Idea of God.* London: Watts & Co., 1931.

*The Apocryphal New Testament.* New York: Peter Eckler Publishing Co., 1927.

Arnold, Sir Edwin. *The Light of Asia.* London and New York: George Routledge & Sons, 1879.

Barnes, Harry Elmer. *The Twilight of Christianity.* New York: Vanguard Press, 1929.

Brown, Robert, Jr. *Stellar Theology and Masonic Astronomy.* New York: D. Appleton & Co., 1882.

Budge, Sir E. A. Wallis *Amulets and Talismans.* New Hyde Park, New York: University Books, 1928.

————*The Gods of The Egyptians.* 2 vols. London: Methuen & Co., 1904.

————*A History of Ethiopia.* 2 vols. London: Methuen & Co., 1928.

————*Osiris: The Egyptian Religion of The Resurrection.* 2 vols. New Hyde Park, New York: University Books, 1961.

Busenbark, Ernest. *Symbols, Sex and The Stars.* New York: The Truth Seeker Co., 1949.

Calverton, V. F. *The Making of Man: An Outline of Anthropology.* New York: Modern Library, 1931.

Carpenter, Edward *Pagan and Christian Creeds.* New York: Harcourt, Brace and Co., 1920.

Carus, Paul. *A History of The Devil.* Chicago: Open Court Publishing Co., 1900.

Christian, Paul. *The History and Practice of Magic.* 2 vols. New York: Citadel Press, 1969.

Churchward, Albert. *The Origin and Evolution of Religion.* London: George Allen & Unwin, 1924.

———*The Signs and Symbols of Primordial Man.* 2d ed. London: George Allen & Co., 1913.

Cooke, Harold P *Osiris: A Study in Myths, Mysteries and Religion* London: The C. W Daniel Co., 1931.

Cutner, Herbert. *Jesus: God, Man or Myth?* New York: The Truth Seeker Co., 1950.

David-Neel, Alexandra. *Initiations and Initiates in Tibet.* New Hyde Park, New York: University Books, 1959.

———*Magic and Mystery in Tibet.* New Hyde Park, New York: University Books, 1965.

Diodorus Siculus. *Library of History.* Translated by C. H. Oldfather. Vols. I & II. Loeb Classical Library. Harvard University Press, 1933, 1935.

Doane, Thomas William. *Bible Myths and Their Parallels in Other Religions.* New Hyde Park, New York: University Books, 1970.

Dupuis, Charles F. *Dupuis' Explanation of An Apocalyptic Work.* Translated by Gilbert Vale. New York: 1849.

———*The Origin of All Worship.* New Orleans, 1872.

Feldman, Burton and Robert D. Richardson. *The Rise of Modern Mythology.* Bloomington: Indiana University Press, 1972.

Findlay, Arthur. *The Psychic Stream.* London: Psychic Press, 1947.

Forlong, J. G . R. *Rivers of Life.* London: Bernard Quaritch, 1883.

Forsyth, David. *Psychology and Religion.* London: Watts and Company, 1935.

Frazer, Sir James George. *Attis, Adonis, Osiris.* New Hyde Park, New York: University Books, 1961.

————*Folklore in The Old Testament.* Abridged edition. New York: Hart Publishing Co., 1975.

————*The Golden Bough.* Abridged edition. New York: The Macmillan Co., 1949.

————*Man, God and Immortality.* London: Macmillan and Co., 1927.

————*The New Golden Bough.* Abridged edition. Edited by Dr. Theodor H. Gaster. New York: Criterion Books, 1959.

————*Totemism and Exogamy.* 4 vols. London: Macmillan and Co. 1927.

————*The Worship* of Nature. New York: The Macmillan Co., 1926.

Georg, Eugen. *The Adventure of Mankind.* New York: E. P Dutton & Co., 1931.

Gibbon, Edward. *History of Christianity.* New York: Peter Eckler Publishing Co., 1923.

————*History of The Decline and Fall of The Roman Empire.* Great Books of the Western World. Vols. 40 & 41. Chicago: University of Chicago Press, 1952.

Goodman, George R. Articles in *The Freethinker,* Vol. 85. London: 1965.

Graves, Kersey. *The World's Sixteen Crucified Saviors.* New Hyde Park, New York: University Books, 1971.

Haddon, Alfred C. *The Races of Man.* New York: The Gordon Press, 1975.

Hallet, Jean-Pierre. *Pigmy Kitabu.* Greenwich, Connecticut: Fawcett Publications, 1975.

Hartman, Franz. *The Life of Jehoshua.* Boston: Occult Publishing Co., 1889.

Hastings, James. *Encyclopedia of Religion and Ethics.* 13 vols. Totowa, New York: Charles Scribner & Sons, 1961.

Higgins, Godfrey. *Anacalypsis.* 2 vols. London: Longmans, Green and Co., 1836.

Hocart, Arthur M. *Social Origins.* London: Watts and Co., 1954.

Ingersoll, Robert G. *Selected Lectures.* New York: Willey Book Co., 1938.

Inman, Thomas. *Ancient Pagan and Modern Christian Symbolism* Kennebunkport, Maine: Milford House, 1971.

Jackson, John G. *Introduction to African Civilizations.* New Hyde Park, New York: University Books, 1970.

——*Man, God and Civilization.* New Hyde Park, New York: University Books, 1972.

Jung, Carl G. *Man and His Symbols.* Garden City, New York: Doubleday & Co., 1971.

Keable, Robert. *The Great Galilean.* Boston: Little, Brown & Co., 1929.

Kuhn, Alvin Boyd. *Shadow of The Third Century.* Wheaton, Illinois: Theosophical Publishing House, 1949.

——*Who Is This King of Glory?* Elizabeth, NJ: Academy Press,1944.

Lugard, Lady. *A Tropical Dependency.* London: Frank Cass & Co., 1964.

McCabe, Joseph. *The Story of Religious Controversy.* Boston: The Stratford Co., 1929.

Massey, Gerald. *Ancient Egypt, The Light of The World.* 2 vols. London: T. Fisher Unwin, 1907.

—— *The Historical Jesus and The Mythical Christ.* Springfield, Massachusetts: Star Publishing Co., 1886.

——*Lectures.* New York: Samuel Weiser, Inc., 1974.

——*The Natural Genesis.* 2 vols. London: Williams and Norgate, 1883. Reissued, New York: Weiser, 1974.

Mbiti, John S. *African Religion and Philosophy.* Garden City, New York: Anchor Books, 1970.

Mead, G. R. S. *Did Jesus Live 100 B.C.?* New Hyde Park, New York: University Books, 1968.

———*Fragments of A Faith Forgotten.* New Hyde Park, New York: University Books, 1960.

———*Pistis Sophia, A Gnostic Gospel.* London: 1896.

———*Thrice-Greatest Hermes: Studies in Hellenistic Theosophy and Gnosis.* 3 vols. London: 1906.

Olcott, William Tyler. *Starlore of All Ages.* New York: G. P. Putnam Sons, 1911.

———*Sunlore of All Ages.* New York: G. P. Putnam Sons, 1914.

Perry, W. J. *The Children of The Sun.* New York: E. P. Dutton, 1923.

Raglan, Lord. *The Temple and The House.* New York: W. W. Norton and Company, 1964.

Rhys, Jocelyn. *Shaken Creeds: The Virgin Birth Doctrine.* London: Watts and Company, 1922.

Robertson, John M. *Christianity and Mythology.* London: Watts and Company, 1936.

Rylands, L. Gordon. *The Beginnings of Gnostic Christianity* London: Watts and Company, 1940.

St. Clair, George. *Creation Records Discovered in Egypt.* Studies in The Book of The Dead. London: David Nutt, 1898.

Sharpe, Samuel. *Egyptian Mythology and Egyptian Christianity* London: J. R. Smith, 1863.

Smith, George. *The Chaldean Account of Genesis.* New York: Scribner Armstrong & Co., 1876.

Spivey, Thomas Sawyer. *The Last of The Gnostic Masters.* Beverly Hills, California: 1926.

Sykes, Egerton. *Everyman's Dictionary of Non-Classical Mythology,* 3d Edition. London: J. M. Dent & Sons, 1968.

Taylor, Rev. Robert. *The Devil's Pulpit.* New York: Gilbert Vale, 1849.

Tompkins, Peter. *Secrets of The Great Pyramid.* New York: Harper and Row, 1971.

Vail, Reverend Charles H. *The World's Saviors.* New York: McCoy Publishing Co., 1914.

Verrill, A. Hyatt and Ruth Verrill. *America's Ancient Civilizations* New York: Capricorn Books, 1967.

Volney, Count Constantine Francis. *The Ruins of Empires.* New York: Peter Eckler, 1890.

Weigall, Sir Arthur. *The Paganism in Our Christianity.* New York: G. P. Putnam Sons, 1928.

White, Andrew Dickson. *A History of The Warfare of Science with Theology in Christendom.* 2 vols. New York: D. Appleton and Co., 1896.

Williamson, W. *The Great Law A Study of Religious Origins.* London: Longmans, Green and Co., 1899.

# INDEX